MESSI
NEYMAR
RONALDO

MESSI
NEYMAR
RONALDO

HEAD TO HEAD WITH THE
WORLD'S GREATEST PLAYERS

LUCA CAIOLI

ICON

Published in the UK and USA in 2016 by
Icon Books Ltd, Omnibus Business Centre,
39–41 North Road, London N7 9DP
email: info@iconbooks.com
www.iconbooks.com

Sold in the UK, Europe and Asia
by Faber & Faber Ltd, Bloomsbury House,
74–77 Great Russell Street, London WC1B 3DA or their agents

Distributed in the UK, Europe and Asia
by Grantham Book Services,
Trent Road, Grantham NG31 7XQ

Distributed in Australia and New Zealand
by Allen & Unwin Pty Ltd,
PO Box 8500, 83 Alexander Street,
Crows Nest, NSW 2065

Distributed in South Africa
by Jonathan Ball, Office B4, The District,
41 Sir Lowry Road, Woodstock 7925

Distributed in India by Penguin Books India,
7th Floor, Infinity Tower – C, DLF Cyber City,
Gurgaon 122002, Haryana

Distributed in Canada by Publishers Group Canada,
76 Stafford Street, Unit 300, Toronto, Ontario M6J 2S1

Distributed in the USA
by Publishers Group West,
1700 Fourth Street, Berkeley, CA 94710

ISBN: 978-178578-111-7

Typeset in New Baskerville by Marie Doherty

Printed and bound in the UK by Clays Ltd, St Ives plc

About the author

Luca Caioli is the bestselling author of *Messi, Ronaldo* and *Torres*. A renowned Italian sports journalist, he lives in Spain.

Contents

Introduction

Who is the greatest of them all? The best in the world? We are always asking that question. It is part of the culture of football, the collective history of lovers of the beautiful game.

It is a question that has divided and continues to divide experts, fans and entire generations. We relish any opportunity to compare and analyse – style, movement, a great play, a free kick, an assist, a goal, a match, a tournament, a World Cup, a Ballon d'Or win. We revel in opinion polls in the papers, on news sites and blogs, and pore over results and statistics. We delight in endless debates. Opinion is divided between rival fans, admirers and detractors, different nationalities. And because the collective footballing memory is a fundamental part of the experience, there is always something that evokes another player, another league, another era. This is part of the charm of being just another link in the footballing chain, this constant oscillation between present and past, without which the game would lose something of its fascination.

Who is the best? Pelé or Maradona, Di Stéfano

or Cruyff, Zidane or Platini, Ronaldo Luís Nazário de Lima or Van Basten? It's a question that has been asked thousands of times, in print, on the radio, on TV. It's a debate that draws in everyone from coaches, players and pundits to the man on the street. Everyone has their own taste, their own opinion, their own idol.

Now the debate centres around Lionel Messi, Cristiano Ronaldo and Neymar da Silva Santos Júnior. Who is the best of the three? Is Messi better than Maradona? Can Cristiano outdo Eusebio? Will Neymar ever overtake Messi, or rise to the heights of fellow countryman 'O Rei' Pelé?

While there may not be a definitive answer to be found in these pages, there is plenty of room for opinions and analysis of the three players' journeys to stardom, their style and abilities, their achievements both on and off the pitch, their similarities and differences. The idea is simply to present the facts and figures – the key to unlocking the stories behind the three best footballers in the world. Then you may draw your own conclusions.

Chapter 1

Childhood

On 23 June 1987 Celia Cuccittini is admitted to the maternity ward at the Garibaldi hospital in Rosario, Argentina. The Messi-Cuccittinis' two sons – Rodrigo, seven, and Matias, five – stay at home with their grandmother, while Jorge Messi accompanies his wife to the hospital. After two boys he would have liked a girl, but the chromosomes dictate that they are to have another boy.

The pregnancy has been uneventful, but during the final few hours complications arise. Gynaecologist Norberto Odetto diagnoses severe foetal distress and decides to induce labour to avoid any lasting effects on the baby. To this day, Jorge can recall the fear of those moments, the panic he felt when the doctor told him that he was going to use forceps, his plea that he do everything possible to avoid using those pincers, which worried him greatly after hearing horror stories about deformity and damage to new babies. In the end the forceps are not needed.

A few minutes before six in the morning on

24 June, Lionel Andrés Messi is born, three kilos in weight and 47 centimetres long, as red as a tomato and with one ear completely folded over due to the force of labour – anomalies which, as with many other new-borns, disappeared within the first few hours. After the scare comes happiness: the new arrival is a little bit pink, but healthy.

On Tuesday 5 February 1985 at 10.20am in the Cruz de Carvalho Hospital in Funchal, capital of Madeira Island, Portugal, Cristiano Ronaldo dos Santos Aveiro is born. He is 52 centimetres long and weighs four kilos. A fourth child for María Dolores dos Santos and José Dinis Aveiro, younger brother to Hugo, Elma and Katia. It was an unplanned pregnancy, nine years after the birth of Katia, and now there is the issue of what to name him. 'My sister, who was working in an orphan-age at the time, said that if it was a boy we could name him Cristiano,' recalls Dolores. 'I thought it was a good choice. And my husband and I both liked the name Ronaldo, after Ronald Reagan. My sister chose Cristiano and we chose Ronaldo.'

Seven years later on the very same date, 5 February 1992, Neymar da Silva Santos is born at 2.15am in Mogi das Cruzes in São Paulo, Brazil. Nadine Gonçalves' waters had broken the day before and she had been admitted to Santa Casa de Misericordia, a huge white and blue building nestled between the narrow lanes of the city centre. It's a natural birth, no complications. He weighs 3.8 kilos, and both mother and baby are doing well. Neymar's parents didn't know they were having a boy – the prenatal scan was too pricey.

At first they are looked after by Doctor Luiz Carlos Bacci – no longer alive today – and then later discharged by Benito Klei. Klei is a União fan, and he knows the baby is the son of a União player. But it is only years later, upon seeing the birth certificate again, that he will realise he helped bring a Barcelona superstar into the world.

So, what to call the little guy? The parents haven't decided on a name for their firstborn. At first Nadine proposes Mateus, and his father agrees. They test it out for a week, but they're not convinced. Finally, when Neymar senior goes to register his son, he changes his mind and opts for his own name: Neymar, with the addition of 'Júnior'. The family will all come to call him 'Juninho'.

Lionel 'Leo' Messi, Cristiano Ronaldo and Neymar Júnior are all born into humble families.

Jorge Messi is the head of department at steel manufacturer Acindar, in Villa Constitución, some 50 kilometres outside Rosario. Mother Celia works in a magnet manufacturing workshop. They own their own home, which Jorge built over many weekends with his father Eusebio on a 300-square-metre plot of family land. It's a two-storey, brick building with a backyard, in Las Heras, a neighbourhood of humble, hardworking people in the southern part of Rosario.

The three-bedroom concrete council house where Cristiano was born no longer exists. In 2007, the house at 27A Quinta do Falcão, in the Santo António neighbourhood of Funchal, was demolished to avoid problems with squatters. On many occasions Cristiano's mother has to go to the town council for bricks and mortar to repair the leaks in the property after a storm. Money is tight in the Aveiro family. Dinis is a gardener for the council, while María Dolores works as a cook so that she can ensure her kids get meals every day. Like thousands of other Portuguese citizens, she had emigrated to France at the age of twenty, where she spent three months cleaning houses in Paris. Her husband intended to join her but was unable to, and she had to return to Madeira.

Neymar's father is a professional footballer for União Mogi das Cruzes Futebol Club, a team in Mogi das Cruzes that plays in the São Paulo state A3 league. The salary is nothing special, but it's enough to live on fairly comfortably. The club also pays the rent on a modest condo at 593 Ezelindo da Cunha Glória Road, in the Rodeio neighbourhood, three kilometres from the city centre. It is here that Neymar Júnior spends the first few years of his life, together with Nadine, who is a housewife.

There is not a lot of money to spare in any of the three families, but all ensure that their children have happy childhoods. Football is, naturally, a recurring theme.

'One Christmas I gave Cristiano a remote-controlled car, thinking that would keep him busy,' recalls Fernão Sousa, the Madrid player's godfather. 'But no – he preferred the football. He slept with his ball, it never left his side. It was always under his arm – wherever he went, it went with him.'

One of Ronaldo's teachers, María dos Santos, remembers her former pupil as 'well behaved, fun and a good friend to his classmates'. When asked about his favourite pastime, she says: 'From the day he walked through the door, football was his favourite sport. If there wasn't a real ball around for him and his friends, they would make one out of socks. He would always find a way of playing football in the playground.'

It was football in the playground and football in the street. 'When he got home from school, I used to tell him to go to his room and do his homework,' says Dolores. 'He always told me he didn't have any. So I would go and start the cooking and he would chance his luck. He would climb out the window, grab a yoghurt or some fruit, and run away with the ball under his arm. He'd be out playing until 9.30 at night.' As if that wasn't enough, he began to skip classes to go out and play.

As her son would later acknowledge: 'I was always playing football with my friends, that's what I loved doing, that was how I spent my time.'

He plays in the street because there is no football pitch in the neighbourhood. One particular street, Quinta do Falcão, proves to be a challenge when buses, cars and motorbikes want to get through. The kids have to remove the stones marking out the goalposts each time and wait for the traffic to pass before resuming the game. The matches they play are intense battles between gangs of friends. They are games that never end. The only hiccup is when the ball lands in one of the neighbours' gardens – and if it's old Mr Agostinho's, he always threatens to puncture the ball.

The football makes plenty of appearances in early photos of Neymar Júnior. He can be seen in a Santos FC shirt from a young age, with a black and white ball under his arm. Nadine remembers a time when she was out buying potatoes in a market, when Juninho was just two years old. He let go of her hand and darted across the street after spying a little yellow plastic ball. And she recalls – as does Neymar himself – that he used to fall asleep hugging a football. Years later, he would come to accumulate 54 balls in his bedroom. His father was amazed when, at barely three years old, rather than grabbing a ball with his hands and saying 'it's mine' like most kids, little Neymar would always retrieve the ball with his feet.

Leo Messi, meanwhile, prefers marbles at the age of three. He wins mountains of them from his playmates and his bag is always full of them. He always has time for round objects, both at nursery and at school. For his fourth birthday, his parents give him a white ball with red diamonds. It is then, perhaps, that the fatal attraction begins. And one day he surprises everyone – his father and brothers are playing in the street and Leo decides to join the game for the first time. On many other occasions he had preferred to keep winning marbles, but not this time. 'We were stunned when we saw what he could do,' says Jorge. 'He had never played before.'

All three players have always been obsessed with the ball. 'The football is the most jealous woman in the world,' admits Neymar. 'If you don't treat her well, she will stop loving you and hurt you. I love her like crazy.'

Chapter 2

The first time

Rosario, Grandoli football ground, a summer afternoon in 1992

'I needed one more to complete the team of children born in '86. I was waiting for the final player with the shirt in my hands while the others were warming up. But he didn't show up and there was this little kid kicking the ball against the stands. The cogs were turning and I said to myself, damn … I don't know if he knows how to play but … So I went to speak to Celia, his grandmother, who was really into football, and I said to her: "Lend him to me." She wanted to see him on the pitch. She had asked me many times to let him try out. On several occasions she would tell me about all the little guy's talents. The mother, or the aunt, I can't remember which, didn't want him to play: "He's so small, the others are all huge." To reassure her I told her, "I'll put him over here, and if they attack him I'll stop the game and take him off."

'So I gave him the shirt and he put it on. The first ball came his way, he looked at it and … nothing.

He's left-footed, that's why he didn't get to the ball. The second time it came to his left foot. He latched onto it and went past one guy, then another and another. I was yelling at him: "Kick it, kick it." I was terrified someone would hurt him but he kept going and going. I don't remember if he scored the goal – I had never seen anything like it. I said to myself, "That one's never coming off." And I never took him off.'

Salvador Ricardo Aparicio – Don Apa, as he is known – tells the story of Leo Messi's first outing on a football pitch.

* * *

São Vicente, Itararé beach, end of 1998
'I went to watch a match between Tumiaru and Recanto da Vila. I was distracted by my son – I turned round to see where he had got to, and I noticed a tiny kid, with short hair and skinny legs. He was running up and down the makeshift stands they had put up for the event. He was running with total ease, as though he were running on a completely flat surface, no obstacles. He never hesitated. His agility and coordination impressed me. It was something rare in such a young, small kid. That's what stood out for me. It was like a light bulb moment, and I asked a friend who he was. He said he was Neymar's son, the guy playing for Recanto who had just missed a penalty. I took a good

look at the father: strong physique and good ball control. I looked at Nadine, the mother, who was there watching: she was tall and slim. It was immediately obvious the kid had good genes. I found myself casually wondering how he would handle the ball.

'Back then I was the coach at Tumiaru. At the end of the match I went over to talk to the father to see if he would let me take him for a tryout. He agreed, and I took the boy over to play. The first time I saw him touch the ball, my heart began to pound as I sensed what a star he could turn out to be. Football was an innate ability for him. He already had his own style, even at six years of age. He had speed and balance and he invented imaginative tricks of his own. He loved to dribble, he knew how to shoot and he wasn't afraid of his opponents. He was different from the others, you could put him in the midst of 200 other kids his age, and even then he would shine.'

Roberto Antonio dos Santos, aka Betinho, delightedly recalls the first time he saw Neymar Júnior, and the discovery of the superstar everyone is talking about.

* * *

Funchal, Andorinha football ground, autumn 1993
'Football was what Cristiano lived for. He was fast, he was technically brilliant and he played equally well

with his left and right foot. He was skinny but he was a head taller than other kids his age. He was undoubtedly extremely gifted – he had a natural talent that was in the genes. He was always chasing the ball, he wanted to be the one to finish the game. He was very focused, he worked equally hard regardless of where he was on the pitch. And whenever he couldn't play or he missed a game he was devastated.' Primary schoolteacher Francisco Afonso, who taught Cristiano's sister Katia, has dedicated 25 years to coaching in the Madeira junior leagues. He was Ronaldo's first coach and he has never forgotten the first time he saw the footballer play.

Neither has Andorinha president Rui Santos: 'A footballer like Ronaldo doesn't come along every day. And suddenly when he does, you realise he's different from all the other kids you've seen play.'

Chapter 3

Fathers

No one can dispute that it's an innate talent, or that football is a true passion for Messi, Ronaldo and Neymar. But what impact have the three stars' fathers had on their education, early choices and decision to make the game they love their profession? And how have they been involved in managing their sons' careers? There is no shortage of stories of famous sports stars whose parents have played a fundamental role through good times and bad.

Iranian-born Emmanuel 'Mike' Agassi was one such parent dedicated to making his son a tennis star. When Andre was just thirteen, his father is said to have modified a machine so that it would serve him tennis balls at 180 kilometres per hour. Car lover José Luis Alonso built a racing kart for his Formula One star son when little Fernando Alonso was just three. And Vietnam War veteran Earl Woods became his son's coach and trainer from the day Tiger could hold a golf club, also at the age of three.

Parents and siblings are the first source of

encouragement, the first captains. Their values, style and passion can become deeply ingrained, and their actions can determine the path of their offspring. In some cases, however, those offspring can feel frustrated that a parent might be trying to fulfil their own dreams through their children.

Let's consider the roles of Jorge Messi, Neymar da Silva Santos and José Dinis Aveiro.

'I loved playing football,' recalls Jorge. 'I used to think about it from the moment I woke up until I went to sleep, and this may well have been passed on to Leo. But I was never one of those frustrated footballers who wanted their child to be a champion at all costs. I never aspired to that. It was my mother-in-law who took Leo to play, not me. Yes, I was his coach for a year at Grandoli, but I didn't act as a personal coach. I enjoyed watching him play – I never imagined he would go so far!

'I was betting on my elder son Rodrigo, who was a good striker. He grew up at Newell's, went on to Central Córdoba and played as a reserve in the first division, but he had a motorbike accident that kept him out for a year. After that he trialled in Chile, and then I took him out to Barcelona to see if he could find a good team in Spain or elsewhere in Europe.'

Jorge Messi might not have been betting on Leo, but he still does everything he can to help his son become a success. He takes him to famed Argentine team River Plate, and then accompanies him to Barcelona so that thirteen-year-old Leo can try out for the youth academy. He wants the best for his son. And when the club wants to sign Lionel, his father takes care of everything. To justify the family having to move to the Ciudad Condal, the club offers Jorge a salary as a match reporter. He has since dedicated himself completely to his son's career, also acting in an advisory role.

'Ever since I was little, he has always told me if I've played well or not after a match. But that's it, he doesn't analyse the rest,' says Lionel. Meanwhile Jorge has been his son's spokesperson, agent and general assistant; he negotiates and agrees contracts, as well as publicity deals.

When Leo's mother Celia and siblings Matías and María Sol have to return to their hometown of Rosario after living in Barcelona, Jorge stays with Lionel. These would be the toughest years for the player, but having his father with him makes things easier. 'We spend a lot of time together, we are friends, although we have our ups and downs,' says Leo.

For Jorge it has meant transition from skilled labourer to manager, under the name of Leo Messi Management: 'It has not been easy, I have had to learn the ropes. I have figured it out along the way. I have had to shield him for his own good from the expectations of people who might do him harm.'

Ironically, he has not been able to shield his son from himself. Jorge is in charge of managing the player's finances, and the Spanish tax authorities believe that not everything is in order. In 2013, the public prosecutor charges him and Leo with failure to declare earnings made through image rights between 2007 and 2009. According to the charges, the Messis owed 4.1 million euros in unpaid tax, a sum which has now been paid up, with interest, to the courts, in the hope of mitigating any punishment. But the payment does not help them avoid a court appearance, which takes place on 2 June 2016, just a few days before the start of the Centenary Copa América. The state attorney is the only one calling for jail time, not only for the father, but for the footballer himself: 22 months and fifteen days, to be exact.

Leo reiterates his position to the judge: 'My father deals with the money, I play the football.' In his fifteen minute statement he insists that 'I trusted my father and the lawyers we had hired to take care of things. At no point did it occur to me that they would dupe me.' Lionel acknowledges that he would go along to a notary's office to 'sign things', without really knowing the details. He kept his enquiries to the bare minimum and his father filled him in only briefly. 'I knew we were signing agreements with sponsors who were giving X amount of money. And that I had to do publicity appearances, photos, that sort of thing. But I have no idea where the money was going.' Jorge confirms this, asserting that the player was not aware of anything. 'We gave him the documents and he signed them.' But the family patriarch is also pleading his own case, insisting that he completely trusted his accountants. According to him, they were the ones who created a corporate structure based in tax havens without Jorge's knowledge, in order to avoid tax on Leo's image rights earnings.

But state attorney Mario Maza is having none of it. 'The man at the top has no idea what's going on. Leo Messi doesn't go to meet the lawyers because he is so focused on his performance. That's what he's paid for and that's what keeps all the FC Barcelona fans happy, including myself,' he says sarcastically. He is convinced the Flea knows more than he was willing to admit, and he makes a scathing accusation. 'I don't want to compare Messi with a "mafioso", but it is as if he was the "capo" of a criminal structure,' he ventures.

While the Messis await the judge's verdict, there is another issue pending which could end up in the courts ... the player's name is one of the first to surface in relation to the so called 'Panama Papers'. According to the leaked information, he and his father formed a shell company in Panama that allegedly served as a tax haven for his image rights deals. The company, called Mega Star Enterprises, was apparently formed just one day after Lionel and his father were separately accused of the 4.1 million euro tax fraud. The family quickly releases a statement denying any wrongdoing. 'The

Panamanian company referred to in the reports is a completely inactive company, which never held open accounts nor funds and which comes from the former company structure put in place by Messi's previous financial advisors, the fiscal consequences of which have already been normalised, with all the income that comes from exploitation of his image rights, prior to and after the procedure carried out in the courts, having been declared before the Spanish Treasury.' For now, the Treasury is investigating the accusations unearthed by the Panama Papers. Their veracity is still unconfirmed. Nonetheless, the player's image has once again been caught up in uncertain financial matters.

* * *

There are interesting parallels in the Neymar family story. Neymar Júnior's father, Neymar da Silva Santos, aka Neymar Pai (Portuguese for 'father'), has a long footballing history. He grew up in the Santos youth team in São Paulo state, before moving to Portuguesa Santista at the age of sixteen where he turned pro. This was the start of his journey through various clubs of modest standing: Tanabi, another São Paulo team, Iturama and Frutal in Minas Gerais state, and Jabaquara, a historic club in Baixada Santista. At 24 he arrived at União Mogi.

'He was a good forward, a number 7,' say his former teammates. 'He played on the edge of the pitch, he was fast, agile, he was a good dribbler, and he was always in the face of the opponent. Above all he was a happy, fun-loving guy, someone who was easy to get on with.' And everyone remembers the birth of Neymar Júnior in 1992: 'Neymar Pai came into the hotel where the team were staying and he was absolutely euphoric. He promised us that one day his son would be the best player in Brazil.'

That Neymar Júnior has achieved so much is undoubtedly due, in part, to his father's support. 'I have got to where I am today because my father has always been by my side,' his son has said in the past. 'He has guided and supported me. I know I can always count on him, that he will always fight for me and my family.'

At 32, with just a single title won in 1997 with Operário de Várzea Grande in Mato Grosso, Neymar Pai retires from football and returns to Santos to begin a new life. He had previously worked as a bricklayer's assistant, now taking up a role as a mechanic. He boosts his income by selling water purifiers, and is a removal man for people in the neighbourhood on the weekends. But he does not lose sight of his son's career, continuing to follow all his matches and offer advice. In 2009 he leaves his job to focus completely on his son. He works alongside football agent Wagner Ribeiro, who represents the player and negotiates and signs contracts, and helps his son through the biggest decisions of his life. First at Santos ... saying no to Chelsea ... then yes to Barça ...

Neymar Pai is by his son's side when Juninho signs the contract at the Nou Camp to join the Catalán club. He guides the activities of NR Sports, his son's management company. Within it, N&N Administration handles financial matters, N&N Store takes care of online business and the sale of products associated with Neymar, and N&N Interests handles any investment. With the help of lawyers, marketing experts and financial advisors, Neymar Pai aims to invest his son's earnings with the aim, he says, 'of securing the future of the next five or six generations of the da Silva Santos family'.

That task has been made easier thanks to the 40 million euro commission invested in N&N by Barcelona as part of the agreement that Neymar transfer to the club a year earlier than originally planned. Meanwhile, 10 million euros were received in 2011 as an option on the player, as well as 2 million over five years to cover scouts' costs. The revelations of the costs of the transfer have provoked debate in both Brazil and Spain, and some have come out in criticism of Neymar Pai. In response, Neymar Júnior has posted a photo and a message to his father on Instagram: 'I want to thank you for the way in which you have overseen my career, for the companies you created to support my work, and the way you have taken care of our family. If I previously played for my favourite team, and now I play for the team of my dreams, I owe it all to you. I know lots of people are talking a lot of rubbish about us ... It's only a matter of time before they realise that you have done nothing wrong ...' He concludes: 'Not only would I die for you, I would give my only son's life for you!'

*   *   *

Cristiano's father José Dinis may not have managed his son's career or fortune, but he was a huge football aficionado and a pillar of support in the player's life. He used to spend his free time as a kit man for local Madeira team CF Andorinha.

When Cristiano is born, he asks team captain Fernão Barros Sousa to take on the role of godfather. Coincidentally, the little boy's baptism takes place on a day marked by football. The ceremony is booked for 6pm at the San António church, but first there's a match at 4pm – Andorinha are playing Ribeiras Bravas, ten kilometres away. Reverend António Rodríguez Rebola is getting nervous. He has already baptised the other children and there is still no sign of either father or godfather. Mother María Dolores and the godmother-to-be are following him around the church, baby in tow, trying to keep the priest calm. Eventually Fernão and Dinis arrive, half an hour late, and the ceremony can finally get underway.

The family are very into their football: Dinis loves

Benfica, while María Dolores adores Luís Figo and Sporting Lisbon. Cristiano soaks up their passion for the game, and begins to go along to the Andorinha ground with his father from a young age. His cousin Nuno, who plays for the club, invites him to come and watch him play and asks whether he wants to join one of the teams. Six-year-old Cristiano decides to give it a go and that's how his adventure begins. His father will go on to follow his career closely, supporting and encouraging him – and convincing him to play on the occasions when he doesn't want to because he thinks his team are going to lose. He tells him only weaklings give up, a lesson little Ronaldo will never forget.

At the age of ten Cristiano signs with Nacional da Madeira. His mother is concerned that he could hurt himself or break a leg playing against much bigger kids. Dinis reassures her: 'Don't worry, they can't catch him, he's too fast.'

Father and son are inseparable until Cristiano goes over to mainland Portugal to join Sporting Lisbon. After that, his mother will be the one to follow him more closely, going with him to Lisbon and later living with him during his early days at Manchester United.

Cut to 6 September 2005. Cristiano is in Moscow. The following day Portugal will face Russia, a key moment in their quest to qualify for the 2006 World Cup in Germany. It is 9pm. Cristiano is in his room watching a film when Portuguese manager Luiz Felipe

Scolari summons him to his room. Team captain Figo is in the manager's hotel suite. Cristiano thinks it's a little odd to be meeting like this, but he suspects nothing. He presumes it must be about some strategic issue, something the coach and the captain want to discuss with him. But they have called him in to inform him of the death of his father. Dinis has passed away at a clinic in London after being hospitalised several weeks earlier.

In July, the father of Man United number 7 had been urgently admitted to Funchal's central hospital with serious liver and renal problems. In an attempt to help save him, Ronaldo requests that he be transferred to England for a liver transplant. But despite improving briefly, Dinis later dies. His untimely death has been caused by alcohol and Cristiano is devastated. 'It was as if our world crumbled around us,' says his sister Katia.

Scolari and the national directors offer Ronaldo the option of leaving Moscow immediately to be with his family. But Cristiano says no, he wants to stay with the team, and he asks Scolari to let him play. 'I wanted to play. That was all I knew how to do,' Cristiano will later explain. 'I wanted to show everyone that I was able to compartmentalise, that I was a consummate professional and that I took my work seriously. I wanted to play that match in honour of my father. I wanted to score a goal for him. I was testing myself and all the people who love me.'

The game against Russia ends in a nil-nil draw and Ronaldo doesn't manage to score the goal that he wanted to dedicate to his father. He will do it at the World Cup in Germany instead, converting the final penalty against England to take Portugal through to the semi-finals. He will raise his hand to the sky and say, 'This is for you, Dad.'

According to friends and neighbours, Ronaldo's father was 'a humble man who got on well with everybody and never had bad words with anyone'. A simple man who had not changed despite his son's success. He maintained the same traditions and friendships that he had enjoyed before anyone knew his name. Although Cristiano had bought him a beautiful home overlooking the ocean and was able to give him every possible luxury, he continued to rise at dawn to help the Santo António newspaper vendor. It was a hobby he never gave up. He would spend the morning with friends at the bar or at CF Andorinha, the club that first nurtured his son's talent. In the afternoon he would catch two buses home.

'My father always encouraged me,' says Ronaldo. 'He always told me to be ambitious and he was proud of my footballing achievements. I love him and I will always love him. He will always be with me. He will always be a role model to me. I like to think that wherever you are you will see what I am doing and what I have achieved.'

Chapter 4

Turning point

A flight over the Atlantic is the common thread that marks the moments Ronaldo, Messi and Neymar's lives would begin to change forever.

It is the Easter holidays of 1997 and twelve-year-old Cristiano has never been on a plane. He has never left his native island of Madeira. He is nervous the night before his flight and he doesn't sleep well. He is on his way to Lisbon for a trial at Sporting, accompanied by godfather Fernão Sousa, who has organised the trial through his various contacts.

Cristiano is convinced he can make it through the trial. He knows he is a good player and will be able to impress the staff. But his nerves and excitement increase when he arrives at the youth team training ground. Coaches Paulo Cardoso and Osvaldo Silva are there to observe him play. They are not particularly impressed by Ronaldo's physique – he's a scrawny little kid. But once they see him in action it's a whole different story. The boy from Quinta do Falcão gets hold of the ball and takes on two or three opponents.

He's relentless – a one man show: feinting, dribbling and driving the ball up the pitch.

'I turned to Osvaldo and I said, "This one's different, he's something special,"' recalls Cardoso. 'And we weren't the only ones who thought so. At the end of the training session all the other boys were crowding around him. They knew he was the best.'

The Sporting coaches are impressed by the trial. They want to see him play again the next day, on the training ground next to the old José Alvalade stadium. This time, youth academy director Aurélio Pereira will be there to observe him.

'He was talented, he could play with both feet, he was incredibly fast and when he played it was as if the ball was an extension of his body,' says Pereira. 'But what impressed me more was his determination. His strength of character shone through. He was courageous – mentally speaking he was indestructible. And he was fearless, unfazed by older players. He had the kind of leadership qualities that only the greatest players have. One of a kind. When they got back to the dressing room all the other boys were clamouring to talk to him and get to know him. He had it all, and it was clear he would only improve.'

On 17 April 1997 Cardoso and Silva sign Cristiano's player identification document. It reads: 'Player with exceptional talent and excellent technique. Of particular note is his ability to dodge and swerve, from stationary or while moving.' Next to 'enrol' there is a tick in the 'yes' box. He plays as a central midfielder, or 'in the hole' as the coaches say. Cristiano Ronaldo dos Santos Aveiro has passed the test – he can play at Sporting. But first they have to reach a deal with his current team, Nacional da Madeira. This time, it's going to cost a little more than twenty balls and a few shirts – the price Nacional paid Andorinha for his transfer.

After a week in Lisbon, Ronaldo returns home to life on the island. It's up to the coaches now to arrange the final details of the transfer. Nacional owes Sporting 4,500 Portuguese 'Contos' (22,500 euros) for Franco, a young footballer who has transferred there from Sporting. Cristiano's signing could be an opportunity to waive the debt, but 22,500 euros for a twelve-year-old kid is an exorbitant price. 'Sporting had never paid anything for a youth player,' says Simões de Almeida, the club's former administrator.

Aurélio Pereira and the other coaches have to convince the administration that it's worth investing so much in one boy. On 28 June Pereira prepares a new report, adding the following postscript: 'Although it may seem absurd to pay so much for a twelve-year-old boy, he has enormous talent, as proven during his trials and witnessed by the coaches. It would be a great investment for the future.' These few lines are enough to win over the club's finance director and the transfer is agreed.

In the last week of August, Cristiano leaves Madeira to settle in to the Sporting youth academy. It's a day the Real number 7 has never forgotten. 'My sisters and my mother were crying. I was crying,' he says. 'Even when I was on the plane and we had just taken off, I thought of my family crying about me and I started to cry again.'

And those first few months in the academy are tough. He finds it impossible to adapt to the locals, life in the apartment with the other players, the rules and the stress of big city life. Everything is different – everything is complicated. Lisbon is another world to him. He is homesick for his family, his island and his friends, and he calls home two or three times a week. He buys a 50-unit phone card and goes down to the phone box. It saddens him to hear his mother's voice, it makes him cry and miss her even more. Dolores tries to cheer him up, telling him to ignore the jokers at school. She often has to console him and convince him that his life and his future are over there in Lisbon, at the Sporting youth academy. 'It was the most difficult time in my sporting career,' recalls Cristiano.

Leo Messi had similar feelings about his first few seasons at Barcelona. 'There were times when my father and I were in Barcelona and the rest of the family was in Rosario. We were suffering. I missed Matías, Rodrigo, my little sister and my mother. I used to cry alone in my house so that my father wouldn't see. Moving from Argentina to Spain was very difficult – I left my hometown, my friends, my people.'

Leo and his father leave Rosario on 16 September 2000 on a transatlantic Aerolíneas Argentinas flight bound for Barcelona. Through football agent Horacio Gaggioli and his colleague Josep Maria Minguella – Barça shareholder number 2292 and transfer advisor to the then club president Joan Gaspart – Leo's agent Fabián Soldini has managed to arrange a trial at *La Masia*, the club's youth academy.

At thirteen Leo is already a well-known figure on the Rosario youth football scene. He plays in the youth leagues with Newell's Old Boys and the local papers dedicate double-page spreads to him. But he has been diagnosed with a growth hormone deficit and has to receive subcutaneous injections every night. It's an expensive treatment, the equivalent of around 12,000 euros a year, which at first is covered by medical insurance and the social security provided by Jorge's employer, Acindar. But according to the Messi family, they stopped covering the total cost of treatment after two years. Seeing the child's promise, the Newell's authorities initially agree to cover part of the costs. But gradually the payments begin to arrive late, and Jorge looks for another solution – first at River Plate and then at Barcelona. At least, that's one of the reasons the family have given for their departure to Spain.

On 17 September, Lionel, Jorge and Soldini arrive in the Catalonian capital. Horacio Gaggioli is waiting for them at El Prat airport to take them to the Plaza Hotel. It has been a particularly turbulent first long-haul flight for the player, and there is not much time to adjust before he has to go and train with the Barça youth team. All the coaches who see him comment that the Argentine kid plays very well, but it is Carles 'Charly' Rexach, the technical director at the time, who must make the decision regarding his future. But he is on the other side of the world, in Sydney, Australia, observing the football tournament at the Olympic Games. Leo will have to wait for him to get back.

On 3 October, Leo is to play in a match between cadets, aged fourteen–fifteen, and first-year students, so that Charly can watch. 'I was coming straight from a meal and I arrived at the ground five minutes late. The two teams were already playing,' recounts Rexach. 'I had to run halfway round the pitch to get to the bench where the coaches were. It took me seven or eight minutes to get all the way round. By the time I sat down on the bench I had already made my decision. I said to Rifé and Migueli [the youth team coaches]: "We have to sign him. Now." What had I seen? A kid who was very small, but different, with incredible self-confidence, agile, fast, technically polished, who could run flat out with the ball, and who was capable of swerving round whoever stood in his way. It wasn't difficult to spot it; his talents, which are now known to everyone, were more noticeable at thirteen. There are footballers who need a team in order to shine – not him. To those who tell me that I was the one who discovered Messi, I always reply, "If a Martian had seen him play they would have realised that he was very special."'

The boss has agreed; the deal is done. Two days later, Leo and his father are on a flight to Buenos Aires. They return home happy. They are assured they will soon be invited back to Barcelona so that the details of the contract can be formalised. But in the final stages things are not so easy. Not everyone at the club is so convinced and when the moment comes to make a decision, doubts arise. Leo is very young, plus he is foreign, and the rules don't allow a foreign child to play in any national league. In addition he has a growth problem that needs treatment, and the club will have to find work for his parents if they move to Spain. The directors ask question after question.

Meanwhile, time ticks on. October and November pass without any decision being reached. On 4 December Minguella calls Rexach. They meet in the restaurant of the Pompey Real Tennis Society in Montjuic. Horacio Gaggioli is also present and he is the most insistent. 'They wanted a written agreement or that was the end of the negotiations,' says Rexach.

'I knew for sure that I couldn't let that kid slip through our fingers, so I grabbed a paper napkin and wrote that I, Charly Rexach, in the presence of Horacio Gaggioli and Josep Maria Minguella, committed to signing Leo Messi if the agreed conditions were met.'

But that's not the end of the story: Rexach now has his work cut out resolving issues with the club and convincing them to pull out the stops for Messi. To start with, he writes a formal report confirming that Leo is an incredibly talented kid. Finally, on 8 January 2001, an agreement is reached and two letters are sent to Jorge: one from Charly, who confirms the sporting agreement made with the family in Barcelona, and the other from club director Joan Lacueva regarding the financial terms. In it he includes details of the house they are to rent, the school, and the 7 million pesetas (around £40,000) Jorge would receive as remuneration for a position at the club, which is as good a way as any of remunerating Leo himself, who would only have been entitled to a study grant. It's enough to convince the Messis to pack their bags.

On 15 February 2001, in the depths of the Barcelona winter, the entire family touches down at the Catalan airport. Leo has not stopped crying during the entire flight. He knows his life is about to change forever.

At just fourteen, Neymar Júnior could have gone through an almost identical transfer experience

to Leo Messi – but to Madrid. He was on the verge
of joining Real, but things didn't turn out quite as
planned. In March 2006, he boards a plane from São
Paulo with his father and his agent Wagner Ribeiro,
who, after much protracted negotiation, succeeded
in helping Robinho del Santos move to the Spanish
capital in 2005.

Neymar Pai was introduced to Ribeiro by Betinho,
the man who discovered and then coached young
Neymar. Ribeiro is convinced of the kid's talents – he
has been helping the family out and has been ready
to take a chance on Neymar since he was twelve. He
has been managing the boy's career together with
Juan Figer – the agent famous for having worked with
Maradona, Gullit, Sócrates, Dunga, Klinsmann and
Kaká.

Ribeiro was in communication with the Santos
board throughout the Robinho transfer and, thanks
to his Real Madrid contacts – strengthened the previous summer – his latest charge has been invited to try
out at the club. They spend three weeks in Madrid,
staying at the branch of the SEK International School
in Villafranca del Castillo, a campus around twenty
kilometres outside the capital where the club sends its
promising young players to study. They are provided
with a car so that Neymar Pai can come and watch the
training matches and tour around the club's sporting
facilities. The medical examinations go well and the

coaches are impressed by Neymar's performance on the pitch.

Jesús Gutiérrez, coach of the youth A team for fourteen-year-old players, remembers that from the very first moment, Neymar 'demonstrated exceptional qualities. He was certainly superior to the other players we had at that time'. And these weren't just any players, they included Dani Carvajal, now in the Real first team, Getafe's Pablo Sarabia, Espanyol's Álex Fernández and Real Oviedo's Fran Sol. But Neymar showed particular talent. 'Everyone agreed we should sign him,' adds Gutiérrez. 'The directors and even the players were unanimous. Generally when someone new comes into the group, there is jealousy. The first thing the others say is: "It's not true, he's not as good as everyone makes out." But with Neymar, they were saying, "Coach, this kid is incredible, he plays like a dream."'

Neymar seems to have slotted into the group and seems happy to be in Madrid. How could he not be? He gets to meet his idols (Ronaldo the Phenomenon, Zidane, Júlio Baptista) and he reconnects with Robinho. On Sunday 26 March he is invited to watch a league match at the Bernabéu: Real versus Deportivo de La Coruña. From the box of honour – closer to the action than the president – he watches the Whites win 4-0, with goals from Héctor, Ronaldo, Sergio Ramos and Júlio Baptista.

Afterwards he is interviewed on Brazilian channel TV Bandeirantes and asked if he enjoyed the game. 'Getting to watch Zidane and Robinho … how could I not have enjoyed it?!' he grins. He also says how much he likes the city and that he wants to stay. Wagner Ribeiro clarifies that 'Neymar has come to visit Madrid because his father could move to Europe, and he could play in Spain, England or Italy. It's just a question of time – he is very talented'. So what does the kid think of that? 'I don't know anything,' he laughs. 'It's those two [he indicates his father and Ribeiro] who know everything. I just play football.'

A few days later, Real have made their decision. The contract is drawn up and both parties accept the terms. It's a five-year contract, with bonus options, school places for Neymar and his sister, and employment for his father. It's just missing his mother's signature. Nadine had a ticket to go to Spain with her son, but she preferred to stay behind with Rafaela. By 29 March, Real has presented their request to sign Neymar to the Madrid Football Federation. The coaches hope he will be able to play in the final few matches of the season. Someone even suggests that he should take part in a youth A team tournament taking place a few days later in Barcelona.

But Neymar will never make it into the squad – instead, he will return to Brazil. There are differing reasons given as to why the deal is never closed. His father cites homesickness, saying his son was becoming more and more down, that he had lost his usual zest for life. He missed his family, friends, his home and his school, the city, Santos and even his favourite dishes – rice, beans and pork. In other words, they were leaving for personal reasons, despite the fact that it would not have been easy to pass up such a significant sum of money.

Others claim that the contract was almost signed, when Wagner Ribeiro asked for 60,000 euros to seal the deal. Most of the directors are said to have been willing, as it's not such a crazy sum. Technical staff secretary Ramón Martínez asks that everything is resolved as quickly as possible. But not everyone is in agreement. 'We have no intention of paying another euro for a kid from Brazil, given all the costs for his family as well,' a director allegedly says. The individual's identity is never revealed, but it now seems that director general Carlos Martínez de Albornoz, the one who has to sign the final agreement, is hesitant to lay out such a sum.

Marcelo Teixeira, president of Santos at the time, disputes this version of events, explaining: 'Upon hearing of Real's offer, we quickly went to great lengths to offer Neymar's parents a five-year contract, a pay rise, and a family home. Both father and son wanted to stay in Brazil, and even before Ney had become a sensation with the Peixe [the 'Fish', as Santos are known], we had presented them with a plan and conditions for his professional career.'

It is not clear whether this was indeed the case, as the new contract with Santos is only agreed some time later, on 13 September 2007. What is clear, however, is that, unlike Messi and Ronaldo, Neymar's foray into European football is now on hold. He returns home to the Peixe, where he will remain until May 2013.

Chapter 5

Club

On 24 June 2016 Leo Messi turned 29 and marked his 16th year at Barçelona – the only club where he has ever played professionally.

His journey began back in the 2004–05 season, when he debuted in an official first team match under the guidance of Frank Rijkaard.

It's 16 October 2004, and Barça are playing the Catalonian derby against Espanyol in Montjuïc. They are winning 1-0 when Leo comes onto the pitch with seven minutes to go to replace goal-scorer Deco. There's some interesting action, but nothing to write home about. At seventeen years and 114 days old, Leo is the youngest player to appear in La Liga for Barça – a record that will later be broken by Bojan Krkić. On 7 December 2004 he gets to play 90 minutes against Shakhtar Donetsk in his Champions League debut. Barça lose 2-0.

1 May 2005 is the 34th match-day of La Liga. The Nou Camp scoreboard indicates three minutes of stoppage time, and Barça are winning 1-0 against Albacete.

Rijkaard brings off Samuel Eto'o, substituting Messi into the unusual position of centre forward. The youngster takes advantage of a ball from Ronaldinho and beats the keeper, Valbuena, with a chip. It's his first goal, and he is the youngest player in the club's history to score in a league game – a record again broken by Krkić, on 20 October 2007 against Villarreal.

On 2 November 2005 Barça are at home to Panathinaikos. Mark van Bommel scores in the first minute, Eto'o scores a hat-trick, and in the 34th minute Messi nets his first Champions League goal to finish the match 5-0.

His first *Clásico* derby against eternal rivals Real Madrid is a few weeks later, on 19 November. Everyone remembers that match because of the standing ovation the Real Madrid fans gave to Barça star Ronaldinho, who scored two goals and put on a stunning performance. But the young Argentine does not disappoint either: he outpaces his marksman, recent Real signing Robinho, he serves up the first goal for Eto'o, and only Íker Casillas's fierce goalkeeping prevents him from scoring one of his own.

22 February 2006. It's the first leg of the final sixteen of the Champions League against Chelsea at Stamford Bridge. When Leo Messi steps onto the pitch, he looks no older than a boy. But he will be the boy of the match. He creates the first real goal-scoring chance and sows the seeds of panic in the Blues' defensive line-up. He's

a nightmare for Del Horno, who will be sent off in the 37th minute after a scuffle with Messi, leaving Chelsea a man down. At the final whistle it's 2-1 to Barça, and José Mourinho has a bone to pick with Leo: 'Am I disappointed with Del Horno's sending off? Did you see the match? Messi put on a good act. Catalonia is a country of culture, you know it is. And I've been to the theatre many times and it's very high quality over there. And Messi has learnt his theatricals from the best …' The response? 'I don't do theatricals,' Leo will say later.

The return leg is on 7 March at the Nou Camp. In the 23rd minute Leo Messi is off, stealing the ball from Robben – but suddenly he puts his hand to his left knee and falls to the ground. He is later found to have a muscular tear in the upper part of his hamstrings – a four-centimetre tear. He will end up being out for 79 long days – and watching the Champions League final against Arsenal at the Stade de France in Paris from the stands. His teammates go on to lift the trophy for the second time in Barça's history. Sad and alone, Leo does not go down to the pitch to collect his medal.

10 March 2007. Another *Clásico* and it's three goals apiece. Leo is Fabio Capello's worst nightmare, the little Argentine who ruins his party. The coach has never won at the Nou Camp – not with Juventus, Roma, nor with his latest club, Real. But this time he was close – until the kid from Rosario popped up, once, twice … bringing the scores level each time, and just when

it looks like it is going the Whites' way, when it looks like they have it in the bag in the 90th minute, Leo pulls the most beautiful sequence out of his hat, the speediest dribbling, a stunning shot: 3-3. Capello and his men are like children who have had their lollipops snatched from their mouths.

It's the morning after 18 April 2007. 'Twenty years, ten months and 26 days later, Messi repeats Maradona's goal,' declares the front page of *Marca*. And it's not the only one. The previous night's Copa del Rey semi-final between Barcelona and Getafe has prompted a flood of headlines, commentaries and word plays, from 'Messidona' to 'the Foot of God', and 'Messi shocks the world'. What has happened? In the 28th minute, Leo has made a 60-metre run, beaten four Getafe players and the goalkeeper, and scored a stunning goal with his right foot. The play instantly brings to mind the goal of the (previous) century, the one scored by Diego Armando Maradona against England in the quarter-final of the 1986 Mexico World Cup. And as if that's not enough, a few weeks later on 9 June, against Espanyol in La Liga, Leo repeats Maradona's 'Hand of God' incident – when Diego beat England goalie Peter Shilton by scoring with his arm. The 'Hand of God' strikes again, and now there is no stopping the endless comparisons between the two Argentine stars.

On 1 February 2009, Leo scores the 5,000th goal

in Barça's Liga history against Racing Santander at the Sardinero. Pep Guardiola is now in the dugout, having replaced Frank Rijkaard after a disappointing 2007–08 season.

The next *Clásico* derby is on 2 May 2009. By now there is no contest, no possible comparison between Real Madrid and Barcelona. The cruel, statistical reality unfolds on the pitch at the Bernabéu: six goals against two – a first. It's the greatest humiliation in the Whites' history. The Blaugrana had never previously scored six goals at the Bernabéu. The closest result was 0-5 in 1974, in Johan Cruyff's day. Guardiola has started to put Messi 'in the hole' behind the strikers, and from there he has netted two of the goals.

A few weeks later on 27 May it's the final of the Champions League, Barça versus Man United at the Olympic Stadium in Rome. And in the 70th minute, Leo ascends to the Roman heavens. In the box, with his back to the defenders, he goes up for the ball after a cross from Xavi, and heads it in at Van Der Sar's far post, taking the score to 2-0 and sealing the victory for Barcelona. The smallest of them all has become the greatest.

It's a case of third time lucky on 19 December 2009. After defeats in 1992 and 2006, Barça beat Estudiantes de la Plata in the final of the Club World Cup, a trophy they have never won in their 110-year history. Messi has scored with his chest, with his heart – bouncing the ball off the Barça emblem on his shirt. He antici-pates his friend Juan Sebastián Verón to score in the 110th minute from a Dani Alves cross. It's 2-1 at the final whistle. The Barça players are crowned kings of the world. They have won the Champions League, the European and the Spanish Supercups, the Copa del Rey, La Liga and now the Club World Cup – no team has ever won six titles in one year, and Messi has been a crucial part of their success.

On 16 January 2010, against Sevilla in La Liga, Messi becomes the youngest player to score 100 goals for Barça at 22 years, six months and 23 days. On 6 April he scores four against Arsenal in the return leg of the Champions League quarter-final, and Gunners boss Arsène Wenger hails him as being 'like a PlayStation'. By the end of the 2009–10 season he has racked up 47 goals, including nine doubles and four hat-tricks. And with 34 of those for Barcelona, he has equalled Brazilian Ronaldo's 1996–97 tally for the club. He has scored more goals than ever since debuting for the first team six seasons ago. But the Champions League is out of reach this time: Barça are knocked out in the semis by José Mourinho's Inter Milan.

Time for another *Clásico*. Since 20 October 2010 Leo has scored in ten consecutive matches. But his run is broken on 24 November against Real at the Nou Camp, despite Barça notching up a 5-0 win. In any case, he serves up two fantastic assists for David Villa.

'King Messi reigns', reads the *Times* headline on 29 May 2011, the morning after Barça's 3-1 Champions League victory over Man United at Wembley. Leo has led a lively, exquisite, lyrical performance, scoring once again, as he did against United in 2009. He has won Man of the Match, and earned the *Guardian*'s comparison with Nándor Hidegkuti's performance at the same stadium, when he scored a hat-trick in Hungary's 6-3 victory over England in the autumn of 1953. 'He is the best player I have ever seen, and will ever see,' says Pep Guardiola after the final. 'We could compete at a very high level, but without him we wouldn't be able to play such a high-quality game. He is a unique and irreplaceable footballer.'

17 August 2011. Messi's two goals in the return leg of the Spanish Supercup against Real Madrid at the Nou Camp, and one in the first leg at the Bernabéu, are enough to win Barça their tenth trophy – and stir up Mourinho, who pokes Guardiola's assistant Tito Vilanova in the eye. Nine days later, Messi opens the scoring against Porto in the European Super Cup, and Cesc Fàbregas finishes the job to add another to the club's trophy cabinet.

Club World Cup final, 18 December 2011. It's Barça 4-0 Santos at the Yokohama Stadium in Japan. Messi unleashes the pain on the Peixe with two goals, and wins the award for player of the tournament. Neymar Júnior, Santos golden boy and Leo's future teammate, will have to console himself with the fact that he has been schooled in a footballing masterclass.

On 18 January 2012 Messi celebrates his 300th appearance for the Blaugrana, the day of Barça's victory over Real in the first leg of a Copa del Rey match at the Bernabéu, the same day as Pep's birthday.

It's 7 March and the final sixteen of the Champions League against Bayer Leverkusen. The score in Germany was 3-1 to Pep's team, and the return looks – on the surface – to be an easy ride. But Messi doesn't care if it's a cinch. He approaches it with the same intensity as ever, and nets five, taking the score to 7-1 at the final whistle. The last person to score five in a European Cup game was Danish footballer Siren Leroy in the 1979–80 season for Ajax against Greek club AC Omnia. No one has done it since the tournament was rebranded as the UEFA Champions League in 1992.

On 20 March, the 29th match-day of La Liga, Leo scores a hat-trick against Granada. With 234 goals in 315 appearances, he is now Barcelona's all-time top goal scorer, overtaking César Rodriguez, centre forward in the 1940s and 50s, who scored 232 in 348 matches over fourteen seasons in a Blaugrana shirt.

On 24 April 2012, Messi steps up to the penalty spot to face Chelsea goalkeeper Pert Čzech in the second leg of the Champions League semi-final. In the first leg at Stamford Bridge, a goal from Drogba broke Barça's concentration and they lost 1-0. The score at the Nou Camp is now 2-1, and this penalty could send them through to the final in Munich. Messi shoots, as Čzech throws himself to his left. But Leo has aimed too high and the ball rebounds off the crossbar. He has missed at the crucial moment. It's the third penalty he has missed out of the thirteen he has taken all season, and his eighth miss out of 34 since he debuted with the first team.

On to the Copa del Rey final, 25 May. Barcelona beat Athletic Bilbao 3-0 in front of a 55,000-strong crowd at the Vicente Calderón in Madrid to take home yet another trophy. It's Pep Guardiola's final match as Barça coach, and Leo has marked the occasion by scoring the second.

On 9 December, Leo scores two to defeat Real Betis in Seville, taking his tally for the calendar year to 86 goals, and beating Gerd Müller's 1972 record of 85. By the end of 2012 he will have scored no fewer than 91 goals. And on 7 January 2013, he becomes the first player in footballing history to win a fourth consecutive Ballon d'Or, the accolade recognised as rewarding the best player in the world. He overtakes legends and three-time winners Johan Cruyff, Marco van Basten and Michel Platini. Barça's number 10 has received 41.6 per cent of the votes, beating Cristiano Ronaldo's 23.68 per cent and Iniesta's 10.91 per cent.

The records continue. On 27 January Leo scores four against Osasuna, taking him to 202 Liga goals, and making him the youngest ever player to break the 200 mark. He beats Telmo Zarra, who scored his 200th goal in 1951 with Athletic Bilbao at 29 years and 352 days. Leo is four years younger.

With his goal against Celta Vigo at the Balaídos Municipal Stadium on 30 March 2013, Leo completes a run of nineteen consecutive goal-scoring matches against every single Liga team – a total of 29 goals in that time. No one in the history of La Liga can lay claim to these sorts of stats. The closest was Brazil's Ronaldo, who scored twelve in ten matches with Barça in 1996–97.

But on 10 April, Leo is out of the starting line-up for the return leg of the Champions League quarter-final against Paris Saint-Germain after he sustained a thigh injury during the first leg at the Parc des Princes. His agreement with coach Tito Vilanova is clear – if he's not needed, he doesn't go on. He will remain on the bench until the 62nd minute. He gets thirteen touches, makes two good passes, runs 2,828 metres, finishes off PSG – who up until that point had been tormenting Barça – and carries them through to their sixth consecutive Champions League semi-final. 'One leg is enough for Messi', proclaims the *El País* headline the following day.

By 23 April he is back in Vilanova's starting line-up to play Bayern Munich at the Allianz Arena. He is on the pitch, but he barely plays. The highest goal-scorer of the last four Champions League tournaments is merely a bystander in this encounter. Messi doesn't seem like Messi – or else Bayern are holding him back. They outstrip him, along with the rest of Barcelona. It ends 4-0, and there are no viable excuses. And in the return leg on 1 May, Messi is out again. He still has not fully recovered from his injury in Paris, and Barcelona are knocked out of the tournament.

Meanwhile, they must focus on La Liga. On 5 May against Real Betis, Messi scores goal number 345, equalling Maradona's career record. Diego scored 345 in 679 matches – 311 in 588 at club level, and 34 in 91 for Argentina. Leo has scored the same in 457 games – 313 in 378 for Barcelona and 32 in 79 for his country.

On 1 September 2013 Messi scores against Valencia at Mestalla, setting yet another record – 100 away goals, beating ex-Real player Hugo Sánchez by one. But on 10 November he is injured in the twentieth minute against Betis in La Liga. It's a relapse of a previous femoral biceps injury in his left leg, which could prove serious. He will not play again for 59 days, until 8 January 2014, when he comes on in the Copa del Rey against Getafe in the 64th minute and manages two goals.

22 January 2014 sees the first leg of the quarter-finals of the Copa del Rey against Levante at the Ciutat de Valencia. Leo Messi has managed four assists, but

he has not scored any goals to mark the occasion of his 400th official match with the *Blaugrana*.

On 16 March he scores a hat-trick in a 7-0 victory over Osasuna, reach 371 goals across all official matches and friendlies and becoming the top goalscorer in Barcelona's history. He overtakes Paulino Alcántara, who scored 369 in 357 matches between 1912 and 1927. Despite this, the club ends the season without hardly any trophies, just the Spanish Super Cup.

The Rosarino's achievements know no limits on 22 November. The twelfth fixture of the season is a night to remember, as the Nou Camp witnesses the number 10 becoming the top scorer in the history of La Liga with 253 goals. He overtakes Telmo Zarra's record of 251, set 60 years earlier, and dedicates the milestone to his son Thiago, and former team-mate Ronaldinho who played a crucial role in his formative years. Three days later he overtakes former Real Madrid player Raúl González as the highest ever Champions League scorer.

But on 4 January 2015, Barça must endure a disastrous match at Anoeta, away to Real Sociedad. Messi is on the bench – not because of an injury, but due to ongoing discord with coach Luis Enrique. They lose, but at least the defeat serves as a wake-up call. From that moment onwards both manager and player make a significant effort to see eye to eye and focus on matters on the pitch. The result? A turnaround that paves the way for the best season in the club's history, winning La Liga and the Copa del Rey in May, and the Champions League on 6 June. It's their second triple in five years, and Lionel finishes a spectacular season in a much more secure position as far as the *Blaugrana* dressing room is concerned.

On 20 December 2015 they play the Club World Cup final in Japan against River Plate. It's the second time in his career he has come up against an Argentine club – previously it was Estudiantes in the Club World Cup final of 2009. 'River are a great team who can compete on a global level, I think it's going to be a good match.' And he doesn't disappoint, guiding his team to victory. He kicks things off the 36th minute, converting a pass from Neymar with the outside of his left boot. Two goals from Suárez in the second half take it to 3-0 at the final whistle, and Barça are crowned the most successful club in the history of the competition.

On 14 February 2016 they at home to Celta Vigo. Leo doesn't know it yet, but it's set to be the most talked about match of the season – and not just because of another stunning scoreline (6-1). He gets Barça off the mark before the half hour with a play that sparks from a dead ball. He later provides an assist to Luis Suárez to go 2-1 up, and he has a hand in the third. If that's not enough to wow the crowds, he'll be back for more with the fourth in the 80th minute. After forcing a penalty, he places the ball on the spot, then takes his run-up, but taps the ball to the side, enabling Suárez to come in and score. It's reminiscent of a strategy used by Johan Cruyff and Jesper Olsen at Ajax in 1982. Some think it's a masterful play, while others think it's disrespectful. Leo steers clear of the debate, instead focusing his attention on the task at hand: winning La Liga.

On 20th April he scores his 500th professional goal. More than 81 per cent of his goals have been scored with his left foot. Twenty-five have come from free kicks, 64 from penalties, and 411 from open play. He has scored 450 with Barça, and the rest with Argentina. He hits the 500th against Deportivo de La Coruña in Riazor, a match with a deluge of Barça goals: 0-8.

And on 14 May the *Blaugrana* beat Granada 0-3 to make it eight La Liga titles in eleven seasons. Messi now has eight league titles, six Spanish Supercups, four Champions League trophies, four Copas del Rey, three European Super Cups and three Club World Cups – all with Barcelona.

* * *

Cristiano Ronaldo dos Santos Aveiro, or 'CR7' as he is now known, cannot quite match Messi in terms of trophies. He has won eighteen titles with his three clubs – Sporting Lisbon, Manchester United and Real. Three

Champions Leagues, two Club World Cups, one FA
Cup, two League Cups, two Community Shields, three
Premier League titles, one Liga, two Copas del Rey,
one UEFA Super Cup and one Spanish Supercup. At
31 years of age, he has played in 671 official matches
across the three clubs, and as of 21 June 2016 has
scored 487 goals.

His first goal in an official match seems an aeon
ago, back on 7 October 2002 when he wore number 28 for the green and white Sporting Lions in the
Portuguese SuperLiga. Sporting, the current title-
holders, are at home to Moreirense. Cristiano has
already debuted in an official match at the Alvalade
on 14 August in the Champions League qualifiers
against Héctor Cúper's Inter Milan. And despite the
nil-nil scoreline, the kid has come away with a thirst
for more. Now coach László Bölöni has put him in the
starting line-up against Moreirense.

It's not a spectacular match. But Cristiano makes
history as the club's youngest ever goal-scorer at seventeen years, eight months and two days. He scores
'a monumental, majestic, unbelievable goal … there
are not sufficient adjectives to describe this young
Sporting prodigy's achievement', scream the SportTV
commentators. It's the 34th minute: Ronaldo gets a
backheel from Toñito just over the halfway line, he
dodges past two defenders, slaloming back and forth
for some 60 metres. He follows it up with a bicycle

kick on the edge of the area to wrong-foot another opponent and slides it smoothly past Moreirense goalkeeper João Ricardo, who makes a desperate dash out into the box. Cristiano tears off his shirt, hugs his teammates and runs towards the stands. Bölöni celebrates with his colleagues in the dugout. But the number 28's performance is not over yet. He goes on to score again, taking it to 3-0 with a spectacular header. The only thing that mars the occasion is when his mother Dolores feels faint in the stands. Perhaps it's the excitement of her son's performance, but in the end it's just a scare. The following day Ronaldo dominates Portugal's front pages with his 'monumental goal'.

Cristiano's performance in the first team has been outstanding. He has become the fans' golden boy. Bölöni has the utmost faith in him, but competition is fierce, with Jardel, Quaresma, João Pinto, Toñito and Niculae already on the strikers' roster. At the end of the season, Ronaldo has played in 25 games and only started in eleven of them. He has scored three goals in the league and two in the cup. Meanwhile, it hasn't been a great run for Sporting, who haven't won any titles.

But Cristiano's first season for the Lions will also be his last. On 6 August 2003 his life will change once again. It's the day the club will officially inaugurate the new Alvalade XXI Stadium, which will later host

Euro 2004 matches. Their opponents for the inaugural match are Manchester United. Meanwhile, Red Devils coach Sir Alex Ferguson, agent Jorge Mendes and Sporting financial director Simões Almeida have come to an agreement. For 15 million euros (£12.24 million) Cristiano will transfer to United on a five-year contract, earning two million euros a year – more than 150,000 a month, compared with the 2,000 euros he has been making at Sporting. At his Sporting farewell match – against his future teammates – the Lions' number 28 shows what he is made of. He amazes everyone with his dribbling, speed, bicycle kicks, change of pace and ability to evade his opponents.

A week later he is on a plane to England, to be presented at Old Trafford on 13 August 2003. United's brand new number 7 is the most expensive teenager in English footballing history. The commentators do not exactly warm to him. They are unimpressed by his casual outfit, his age and, above all, the price that United have shelled out for him. They want to know if he is nervous about taking on the legendary shirt and playing at such a big club in such a competitive league. 'I'm not afraid, not at all,' replies Ronaldo. 'I know it will be difficult, but I will learn so much playing alongside some of the best players in the world.'

He debuts at Old Trafford just three days after his presentation. It's the first match-day of the season and United are at home to Bolton. Cristiano is on the bench, but in the 60th minute Ferguson needs to shake up a game that is stuck at 1-0 and he sends him on as a substitute for Nicky Butt. The spectators stand to applaud the new signing. The 67,647 fans certainly aren't disappointed by his running and dribbling, and by the final whistle he is crowned man of the match and gets to pop his first bottle of champagne. 'It looks like the fans have a new hero. It was a marvellous debut, almost unbelievable,' comments Sir Alex after the 4-0 win.

On 1 October, the number 7 makes his Champions League debut against VfB Stuttgart. And just a month later, on 1 November against Portsmouth at Old Trafford, he scores his first goal in the number 7 shirt from a free kick taken just outside the area. It's a powerful shot, the ball arcs over the defenders and strikers, deflects off the pitch and flies into the net. It's a shot reminiscent of club legend David Beckham. It's a promising start for the boy from Madeira, who by the end of the season has scored eight goals in 39 matches across all competitions. The most important was against Millwall at the Millennium Stadium in Cardiff in the final of the FA Cup – the first of United's three goals, which will win them their only title of the 2003–04 season.

Cristiano's first goal in the 2004–05 season doesn't come until 5 December – against Southampton at Old

Trafford. Ferguson comments that it's the first of the twelve goals Cristiano has promised him. But after 50 matches he has only managed nine. And it's not a great season for United either – no titles this year.

The 2005–06 season, his third with the club, is not easy – either on or off the pitch. He loses his goal-scoring bet with Ferguson again, having said he would net fifteen and only managing twelve. He is definitely progressing, but for the second year running United finish behind José Mourinho's Chelsea in the Premier League. They don't make it past the group stage in the Champions League, knocked out by Benfica, and by December they are out of Europe. Their only trophy this year is the Carling Cup, in which they beat Wigan 4-0. Ronaldo scores the third. Meanwhile, on 29 October 2005 against Middlesbrough, Cristiano has scored the club's 1,000th Premier League goal, although United lose 4-1.

But despite United's lacklustre season, Cristiano has been voted by the fans as the FIFPro Special Young Player of the Year. Teammate Wayne Rooney has won the official prize in the same category, and there has been talk of the two being the protagonists of the upcoming 2006 Germany World Cup. But in the quarter-final Portugal-England match on 1 July 2006 in Gelsenkirken, there is an unfortunate incident that provokes much speculation about Cristiano's future at United.

Things have been fairly uneventful until the 62nd minute, when Rooney tries to make a break for it between Carvalho and Petit. After a bit of a struggle, Carvalho ends up on the ground and Rooney inadvertently tramples him, catching his studs in a rather painful area. The foul triggers a scuffle between the English and Portuguese players. Cristiano is the first on the scene, rushing over to reason with the referee. Rooney gives him a shove and appears to say something like: 'You stay out of it.' In the end, referee Horacio Marcelo Elizondo pulls out the red card, sending the United number 9 back to the dressing room. The English fans are convinced Ronaldo has pressured the ref into sending off Rooney. The British TV channels start to show clips of Cristiano apparently winking towards the Portugal dugout after the expulsion. On 3 July, *The Sun*'s front cover shows a picture of Cristiano's head in the middle of a dartboard, with the headline 'Give Ron one in the eye'. The article reads: 'Here's every England fan's chance to get revenge on the world's biggest winker ... We've made Ronaldo's wink the bullseye. So put it up in your office – and give the sly señor one in the eye.'

Cristiano is concerned – he is afraid of the press and the possible reactions from opposition fans if he returns to play on English soil. He says it will be difficult to return to a country where he is not welcome, and suggests that his dream is to go and play in Spain.

Sir Alex and United chief executive David Gill fly to the Algarve, where the Portuguese has been spending his vacation, and finally persuade him to return to England.

From the beginning of the 2006–07 season, Ronaldo begins to shine, and demonstrate not only the talent but the strength of character he developed during those difficult early years in Lisbon. 'I managed to show that the pressure only makes me stronger,' he will later say. 'I tested myself and I came out stronger.' On 22 April 2007 he is named the Professional Footballers' Association Player of the Year. And this year he will win his first big title – the Premier League. United have regained the English crown after four years of drought, ending the reign of José Mourinho's Chelsea, who won in 2005 and 2006. Ronaldo has played his part – with seventeen goals he is the third-highest scorer in the league, after Chelsea's Drogba (twenty) and Blackburn's Benni McCarthy (eighteen).

The following year in the 2007–08 season he will be the top scorer with 31, beating Adebayor and Fernando Torres, who have netted 24 each. His total across all tournaments is 42. And on 12 January 2008 he scores his first hat-trick for United, against Newcastle. On 18 March Ferguson gives him the captain's armband, and he responds by scoring two against Bolton. He will later go on to score two against Stoke City on 15 November, taking him to more than

100 goals for Man United. Meanwhile, his 2007–08 season achievements include the Charity Shield trophy, his second consecutive PFA Players' Player of the Year award and the Premier League title (United finish with 87 points, two above Chelsea and four above Arsenal).

And, above all, a beaming Cristiano gets to lift the Champions League trophy under a rainy Moscow sky, 40 years after United's first European title win, led by George Best in 1968. For the third time in the club's history they are crowned the kings of continental football – and they have a solid defence and Cristiano's brilliant overall performance to thank for it. The Reds' number 7 has undoubtedly been the star of the tournament, and with eight decisive goals he is the top goal-scorer and player of the tournament. The first of the eight was on 19 September 2007 at the Alvalade against his former team, and the eighth is in the final itself against Chelsea at the Luzhniki Stadium in Moscow. In the 26th minute, Paul Scholes goes past the Blues' defence, Wes Brown crosses and Ronaldo puts a phenomenal header past Petr Čech to make it 1-0. Frank Lampard equalises just a few seconds after half time. After 120 minutes of play the score is still 1-1, and the game goes to penalties.

The third penalty falls to Cristiano, and he tries to throw off Čech with a Brazilian-style *paradinha* – the run-up followed by a little stop just before taking the shot. But the goalie anticipates the move and still manages to block it. The Portuguese buries his head in his hands, devastated. 'I thought it was going to be the worst day of my life,' he will say later. 'But despite my mistake, my teammates still believed we could win. And in the end, it was the happiest day.'

But he won't be able to say the same the following year. The Rome final of the Champions League against Barcelona on 27 May 2009 is the most hotly anticipated match in European football, the best possible line-up with two teams that will undoubtedly put on the best show on the continent. Cristiano is coming off a better-than-average season. He has played in 53 games and scored 26 goals, including eighteen in the Premier League and four in the Champions League. Before coming to Rome, Manchester United retained their spot as kings of England with a four-point lead over Liverpool in the league, and on 1 March they beat Spurs in the League Cup final at Wembley.

It hasn't been as strong a season for Cristiano as the previous one, but he is the current Ballon d'Or winner after beating Messi and Fernando Torres to the prize on 2 December 2008, and he wants to show that he is still the number one, despite the little Argentine's rapid ascent. But in the end it's Messi who wins the duel, scoring the second of Barça's goals to make it a definitive 2-0. It's CR7's final match in a United shirt.

On 6 July 2009 he will be presented as Real Madrid's latest superstar signing at the Santiago Bernabéu in front of 80,000 fans. On 29 August, the first match-day of La Liga, he scores his first goal in an official match against Deportivo de La Coruña at the Bernabéu – a penalty that puts Real in the lead. He celebrates by looking towards the stands and leaping into the air, fist raised. It's a fantastic start, the best of his career, and one of the most stellar debuts in Real Madrid history.

By the end of the season, despite two months out due to injury, Cristiano has scored 33 goals – 26 in La Liga, including his first Real hat-trick on 5 May 2010 against Mallorca – and seven in the Champions League. He has dazzled the crowds at the Bernabéu and all the Real fans. And he has convinced his team-mates and coach Manuel Pellegrini that he is something special. Nonetheless, he feels sad and frustrated that the Whites have not won a single title all year. Real have not made it past the final sixteen in the Champions League, and they have been outdone by Barça in both La Liga and the Copa del Rey. It's a theme that will continue to frustrate.

In 2010–11, Cristiano nets 53 goals across all three competitions, making him the highest goal-scorer in a European league and winner of the Golden Boot. He also beats a Telmo Zarra record, scoring 40 in 34 Liga matches to overtake the Athletic Bilbao star's 38 in 30 in the 1950–51 Liga season, as well as beating Real star Hugo Sánchez's 38 in 35 in 1989–90. But for all his goals, only the one in the final of the Copa del Rey in Mestalla on 20 April 2011 proves decisive. Beating Barça goalkeeper Pinto with an incredible header in the 103rd minute, his spectacular goal clinches Real's sole trophy of the season. But it's not enough for CR7. 'Real aspires to win all the titles and I would have preferred to score half the number of goals but win La Liga or the Champions League,' he says in an interview.

On to 2011–12, where a missed penalty will deny Real Champions League success, but a Cristiano goal at the Nou Camp will help them bring home La Liga. Let's start with the best part of the season, Cristiano's most important goal since arriving at Real.

It's 21 April 2012, Barça versus Real Madrid, 8pm at the Nou Camp. For the first time since La Liga 2008–09, the Whites have made it to the end of the season ahead of the Blaugrana. They are four points clear of Pep's team, 85 to 81, enough to seal the championship at the home of their rivals and end Barça's incredible three-season run. Ronaldo scores the final goal of the 2-1 victory. Mesut Özil gets the ball from Di María in front of the halfway line and crosses deep towards Cristiano. He breaks away from Mascherano and heads towards Víctor Valdés, sending the ball to the right and beating the Barça goalie at the near post. It's an incredible shot, and Cristiano celebrates by running towards the Barça fans, signalling for them to calm down, mimicking the gesture Raúl once made towards them. 'Calm down, calm down, I'm right here,' he shouts, only too aware of what the goal symbolises – a seven-point advantage over Barcelona. Victory in La Liga.

Cristiano faces another challenge in just a few days' time: the return leg of the Champions League semifinal against Bayern Munich, the penultimate step towards getting their hands on their tenth Champions League trophy. The whole of Madrid has been dreaming about it. Cristiano responds by netting the first goal from the penalty spot, and scoring again a few minutes later, giving Real the momentum they need. With Real 2-0 up he moves ten paces back and waits for the Germans to falter so he can go on the counter-attack. He wants to sit it out. It's a conservative strategy from Mourinho, which fails them in the end when Robben scores, taking them on to a penalty shoot-out, where Cristiano misses and Real are knocked out. Cristiano has missed a penalty against Chelsea – just like Leo Messi did in the previous round of the tournament – despite the Portuguese having netted his previous 27 penalties. He takes Real's first in the penalty shoot-out. He sends it to Neuer's right and the German goalkeeper blocks it, before denying Kaká and Ramos as well. Xabi Alonso is the only one who scores. Íker Casillas's two saves make no difference

– the tenth Champions League trophy will have to wait until next year.

On 29 August 2012 at the Bernabéu, Cristiano and the Whites clinch the Spanish Supercup, leaving Messi and Barça in the dust to take home their first trophy of the season. CR7 has scored in both legs. And in the next *Clásico* on 7 October, he scores two more against the Catalans and sets a new record – scoring in six consecutive Real–Barcelona derbies.

By the end of the 2012–13 season he will have chalked up some impressive figures: 55 goals in 55 matches, – 34 in La Liga in 34 games, seven in the Copa del Rey, two in the Spanish Supercup and twelve in the Champions League. He has netted a total of 201 in 199 matches across all competitions since he signed with Real in 2009, making him the sixth-highest goal-scorer in the club's history. In just four seasons he has over-taken great players such as Amancio Amaro, Emilio Butragueño, Pirri and Paco Gento. He has become the highest-scoring Portuguese player in European competitions with 52 goals, beating records set by Eusébio and Real legend Alfredo Di Stéfano. And in the last season he has been the driving force behind Real Madrid, the hero of many matches, the player with the most guts and enthusiasm, who has pulled the results out of the bag. He has become an authoritative leader on the pitch and in the dressing room.

In particular, he has led the team through the

Champions League final sixteen round against Man United in February 2013, scoring two in the first leg – an impressive leap and a stunning header – and one in the return leg to eliminate his former club. It's been a satisfying season, albeit another void of trophies.

Nonetheless, he continues on his goal-scoring mission, and by the end of 2013 he has netted 69 across all matches for Real and Portugal. And on 13 January 2014, he gets the recognition he has been dreaming of since 2008: his second Ballon d'Or. He reclaims the trophy, crying tears of happiness. Just a few weeks earlier he had broken another record. On 10 December at the Parken Stadium in the final Group B Champions League match against Copenhagen he became the first player to score nine goals in the group stages. The 69 goals have been scored across 59 games: an average of 1.16 per game and a new personal best.

Despite the outstanding stats, La Liga is still out of his reach. But Real are victorious in the Copa del Rey, before going on to clinch the title that Cristiano and all the Whites fans have been dreaming of: the Champions League. It's the club's tenth and CR7's second. They lift the trophy on 24 May in his home country, in Lisbon, after defeating Atlético Madrid 4-1.

The following season will end very differently, despite raking in every individual award imaginable (UEFA's Best Player in Europe for the 2013–14 season; Best Player, Best Goal and Best Striker in Spain's

Liga de Fútbol Profesional 2013–14 awards; as well as Globe Soccer's Best Player of the Year.) In fact, everyone seems more interested in his private life than his performance on the pitch. First there's his split with model Irina Shayk, and then there's the controversy caused by his 30th birthday celebrations, held just hours after the Whites' most humiliating defeat since Guardiola's Barça beat them 5-0 in November 2010, when Mourinho was in the dugout. This time, on 7 February 2015, it's a 4-0 whitewash by Atlético, and Cristiano only manages a single shot on target. It's shaping up to be a gloomy season for Real Madrid, void of any of the big titles – no Liga, Champions League or Copa del Rey this year. Ronaldo can console himself with top goal-scorer (he has already scored more than 300 goals for the Whites). One particular performance of note is Real's 9-1 victory over Granada on 5 April, with five by Cristiano. It's the first time he has ever scored five in a match, putting him on track to be crowned the 2014–15 top scorer across all the European leagues for the fourth time in his career, with a total of 48 goals.

A year later, CR7 will reach even greater heights. It hardly matters that 2015–16 is one of the most difficult seasons he has ever experienced, first plagued by a tense relationship with coach Rafa Benítez (replaced by Zinédine Zidane halfway through the season), and then tainted by those who are calling for the club's management to get rid of him. This doesn't stop him becoming the Whites' top scorer in La Liga, with 231 goals, as well as the top goal-scorer in Real Madrid history across all competitions: 324 in 308 matches – an average of 1.05 a game. It's one more goal more and 433 fewer matches than Raúl, who had previously held the record, and who immediately sends him a congratulatory text.

But above all, he will remember 2015–16 for his third Champions League victory. 'I had a vision. I knew I was going to score the winning goal and I said to Zizou, "Leave me till last in the penalty shoot-out because I'm going to score the winning penalty." And that's exactly what happened.' No room for bashfulness as the Portuguese analyses what happened in the final against Atlético Madrid in Milan on 28 May. It's decided in the Russian Roulette of the penalty shoot-out, but he's the last one to step up, and his goal is worth the Champions League trophy. The number 7 is the top scorer of the tournament with sixteen goals, nearly double that of Bayern Munich striker Robert Lewandowski, who is second with nine. Barça's Luis Suárez has snatched the La Liga top-scorer and Golden Shoe awards from Cristiano this year, but when it comes to the Champions League no one comes close.

* * *

Neymar has had similar success when it comes to breaking records. Despite his age, the Brazilian has a wealth of awards and achievements under his belt.

Here's how it all began. On Saturday 7 March 2009 Santos are playing Oeste de Itápolis in the 'Paulistão' – the Paulista State Championship. There is a 22,000-strong crowd, most of them Peixe fans. And they have all come to watch a seventeen-year-old kid make his first team debut. Coach Vágner Mancini calls upon Neymar in the 58th minute, offers him some last-minute advice and sends him onto the pitch to replace Colombian midfielder Mauricio Molina. Before long, he makes a run into the right-hand corner of the area, dodges away from his opponent and takes a fierce shot, which ricochets off both crossbar and post. Impressive stuff for a first touch.

His first goal comes eight days later at the Pacaembu municipal stadium – a header that puts Santos 3-0 up against Mogi Mirim. Neymar points to the sky before jumping and punching the air with his fist, imitating Santos's greatest hero, Pelé. 'I celebrated like that because I have been inspired by Pelé. I promised my father that's what I would do,' explains Neymar at the final whistle. It's also in honour of his paternal grandfather Ilzemar, a huge Pelé fan, who made his grandson watch videos of O Rei's goals over and over. And while his little cousins were playing with dolls, Neymar would go to the park and play ball with his grandfather. Ilzemar died in 2008 without having seen his grandson play for Santos, so the celebration pays tribute to him, and is also a special moment for Neymar Pai.

After leaping into the air, he goes over to hug Paulo Henrique, who has been his friend and team-mate since they played in the Under 20s together. 'This Santos kid is on fire!' cries Sport TV commentator Milton Leite. 'This could be a historic goal! This could be an important date in the history of Brazilian football!'

And he's not wrong, because in less than a year Neymar is to become the star of Santos, the team with whom O Rei Pelé dominated in the late 1950s and 1960s.

On 14 April 2010 against Guaraní in the final sixteen of the Copa do Brasil, Neymar nets no fewer than five goals, each more stunning than the last. In the second minute, he converts a penalty after a *paradinha* run-up and stop. In the 30th minute it's a left-footed shot from inside the area. In the 38th he beats the goalie after a cross from Arouca. In the 81st Robinho crosses from the left, and the number 11 needs just two touches to score his fourth. And finally in the 85th, Madson sets off like a rocket, passes to Robinho, who flicks it to Neymar, who doesn't miss. It's Santos 8-1 Guaraní at the close.

Neymar has won over the fans – not just with his

avalanche of goals and excellent performance, but with his sense of fun, his desire to enjoy himself while playing football. And with that joy come his first two title wins. First, the Paulista Championship. The final is against Santo André and the Peixe win the first leg 3-2. The sun hasn't been shining on Neymar, and he is substituted at half time. On 2 May 2010 they play the return leg at the Pacaembu, and this time the number 11 scores two goals. The first is a true work of art: Robinho serves it up in the middle of the box, Neymar dodges round two defenders and the goalkeeper, and shoots right in front of goal. It's reminiscent of Pelé. After scoring his second, he takes a break, substituted by Roberto Brum. But Santo André will not give up, and in the end they are 3-2 up. The match gets more complicated after three sending offs in the Santos ranks, and with only eight men on the pitch they have to do everything in their power to stay afloat. The final whistle goes after an agonising finish for both the players and the fans, and the score remains 3-2 to the visitors. It's a draw across both the legs, but Santos are declared victorious for their overall performance throughout the tournament. Neymar cries as he receives his medal. Next up it's the Copa do Brasil on 4 August, where Santos beat Vitoria. Neymar is the highest goal-scorer of the tournament with eleven. In the Paulistão he had scored fourteen. He is the country's newest idol.

But five weeks later he has a fall from grace. On 15 September 2010 Santos are playing Atlético Goianiense at home at the Vila Belmiro in the 22nd match-day of the Brasileiro Championship. Five minutes before the final whistle Neymar goes down in the box – penalty. He collects the ball and is preparing to place it on the spot when Léo, the Santos number 3, comes over to tell him the coach has decided that Marcel should take the shot. Neymar lets the ball drop, holds out his arms and turns to the dugout, unleashing some choice words in the direction of coach Dorival Júnior. After the match, Goianiense coach René Simões calls Neymar a monster. The following day the incident is the subject of countless debates on television, and stirs up plenty of discussion between pundits, columnists and fans. The papers are full of talk about bad boy antics, and it's a difficult time for the young forward. He says that if not for family, loyal friends and the club's support, he might have considered quitting football forever. In the end it's Dorival Júnior who leaves, but it's an episode that will leave its mark on the Peixe player, and ultimately help him to grow and mature.

By contrast, 2011 is a stellar year. On 15 May Santos win the Paulista cup at the Vila Belmiro for the second year running, thanks to Neymar's crucial goal in the return leg against Corinthians. On 2 June, 46 years after Coutinho and Pelé's goals against Argentina's

Boca Juniors, and 48 years after Caetano's own goal and Pelé's double against Uruguayan team Peñarol, Santos finally reclaim the Copa Libertadores – beating Peñarol once again, thanks to another spectacular Neymar performance in the return leg at the Pacaembu. And against Ronaldinho's Flamengo on 27 July he scores a stunning goal that will later win him the Puskás prize for goal of the year. The one big disappointment of his year comes in the FIFA World Club Cup on 18 December in Yokohama, when his dream of repeating Pelé and Co's 1963 victory in the competition – then known as the Intercontinental Cup – is crushed when Barcelona make mincemeat of the Peixe. The only silver lining is that Neymar gets to take home Leo Messi's shirt.

On 5 February 2012, Neymar celebrates his forthcoming twentieth birthday by scoring his first goal of the year – and his 100th career goal, against Palmeiras at the Prudentão stadium. He has netted 82 for Santos and eight for Brazil, plus nine with the Under 20s and one with the Under 17s. And on 29 April against São Paulo he scores his 100th Santos goal, three years and 51 days after his debut, entering the hall of fame of the greatest Santista goal-scorers. And there are more team triumphs to come: in their centennial year, Santos are Paulista champions for the third year in a row, thanks to another Neymar double in the first leg of the final against Guaraní. Forty-three goals, three-time champions, victory in the South American Recopa – not to mention an avalanche of individual awards, including, for the second year running, the South American Footballer of the Year award, as chosen by Uruguayan newspaper *El País*. In short, 2012 has been a great year for both Neymar and Santos.

The following year it is time to bid farewell to friends and teammates, to the club where he has grown up and gained idol status, and to the fans who have cheered and applauded him from day one. On the first match-day of the Brasileiro Championship, Sunday 26 May 2013, against Flamengo at the newly inaugurated Mané Garrincha Stadium in Brasilia, Neymar da Silva Santos Júnior plays his final match in a white shirt. Nine years after his journey began in the Peixe youth leagues, five years after his official debut, 299 appearances, 138 goals and six titles later (three Paulistãos, one Copa do Brasil, one Copa Libertadores and one Recopa Sudamericana), the kid from Mogi das Cruzes is off to Europe, to join the ranks of FC Barcelona.

His new adventure begins at his Nou Camp presentation on 3 June. After that it's full speed ahead: an 8-0 win against his old club in a friendly on 2 August, his Liga debut on 18 August against Levante, his first goal in an official match on 21 August in the Spanish Supercup against Atlético Madrid, the ultimate first test against Real Madrid on 26 October, his injury against Getafe in January 2014, and 'Neymargate' – the controversy over his signing.

It's a season of adjustment for the youngster in every sense: a new life far from his home country, and a very different style of play. And on top of that, things are not going the team's way – it's one of their worst seasons in recent memory.

But 2014–15 will be very different. He forms an incredible bond with Leo, and Barça walk away with the triple. *Marca* calls the Brazilian 'this season's sensation for Barcelona'. He already feels an affinity with the *Blaugrana*. 'This is undoubtedly the best moment in my career. My greatest match. I'm sure this day will go down in history,' says an emotional Neymar, after beating Juventus to the Champions League trophy on 6 June 2015 in Berlin. And he has achieved something no one else has: winning a Champions League and a Copa Libertadores, and scoring in both finals. In his second year at Barça, the Brazilian has played in 50 matches, 4,152 minutes in total, and has scored 38 goals. Ten of these are in the Champions League – equal to Leo Messi and Cristiano Ronaldo. All three share the Pichichi award for top scorer in the tournament. Ney is already up there with the greats.

And he's back at it the following season, as 2015–16 sees him cement his star status. The achievements at club level are not quite as spectacular as the previous year – although they still win La Liga and the Copa del

Rey – but individually, Ney is on fire. During most of the first part of the season he takes the reins following Messi's injury, and at various points he is the leading goal-scorer of the championship, albeit temporarily. Towards the end of 2015 Barcelona are in the running for the Club World Cup, a particularly special tournament for the Brazilian, not just because of its fame among South American fans, but because it was his chance to win one after suffering a 4-0 whitewash in the 2011 final with his Brazilian club Santos, at the hands of Guardiola's Barcelona. This time his team has the edge. On 20 December they beat River Plate 3-0 in the final. Ney doesn't score but he provides an assist for Messi. And now he has won one of the few titles that had previously eluded him. Just three years after arriving at Barcelona he has notched up two Ligas, two Copas del Rey, one Champions League, one European Super Cup and one Club World Cup.

Chapter 6

Country

They are the stars of their squads, the leaders of their national teams, and each one carries the hopes of their nation in every big tournament.

But the journey to triumph with Brazil, Argentina and Portugal have been very different – right from their respective debuts. Neymar's first match is a joyous occasion, Messi's is unlucky and Ronaldo's is more comfortable.

Neymar's debut with the Brazilian Canaries is on 10 August 2010 against the United States in New Meadowlands, New Jersey. Manager Dunga has been dismissed following the South Africa World Cup, and the Brazilian Football Federation has picked Mano Menezes to replace him. The new boss has won three titles in three years at the Corinthians: the 2008 championship in the Brazilian second league, which helped the team move up to the top league, followed by the Paulista championship and the Copa do Brasil in 2009. It augurs well for his new role.

Neymar is called up for the game against the US.

Dunga hadn't taken him to South Africa, and the whole country has been waiting to see his name on the call sheet. He'll be wearing number 11, the same as at Santos, and by the end of the match he will be brimming over with happiness. He was not expecting to score on his debut with the big boys, much less with a header, but that's exactly what he has succeeded in doing in the 28th minute.

Robinho passes to André Santos, who pushes forward down the left-hand side. He crosses, and Neymar anticipates the defender before heading it to the right of goalkeeper Howard. The kid from Mogi das Cruzes drops to his knees, throws his arms in the air and then kisses the Brazilian emblem before being piled upon by Ganso and Alexander Pato. 'My goal helped us to feel more calm – after that everything went smoothly,' Neymar says later, admitting that after a debut like that, any nerves he might have felt in the build-up have long since melted away.

Meanwhile, Leo Messi's debut with the senior Argentine team is on 17 August 2005, during a friendly against Hungary in Budapest, at the stadium dedicated to Ferenc Puskás. He comes on for Maxi López in the 65th minute. And he is on the pitch for little more than 40 seconds. On his second touch, he dribbles the ball past Vanczák. The Hungarian grabs him by his brand-new number 18 shirt; Messi lifts his arm and pushes him back. Bam! He catches the defender full in the face. German referee Markus Merk is in no doubt. He elbowed him. And he pulls out the red card in front of the disbelieving Argentines. Sent off in his first match. Not the scenario Leo had imagined. He is to spend the rest of the match crying. His coach and teammates think the referee's decision is excessive, but their words of consolation are in vain.

On 14 August 2003 Cristiano Ronaldo receives a call from his mother informing him of his first call-up for Portugal's friendly against Kazakhstan. Shortly afterwards, his agent Jorge Mendes confirms the good news. Ronaldo is happy and proud, albeit a little over-whelmed. 'This is a very special moment in my life, all the good things have come at once – first Man United and now the national team,' he says. 'I want to play and I want to win.' On 20 August 2003 in Chaves, Portugal, Ronaldo dons the red and green shirt for the first time. Luiz Felipe Scolari brings him on in the second half, replacing Luís Figo. He suddenly finds himself surrounded by the champions he has always looked up to. His mentors Figo and Rui Costa have told him to stay calm and play the way he always does. Above all, they tell him not to let his emotions get the better of him. The youngster follows their advice to the letter and the press later name him player of the match. Scolari congratulates him.

* * *

Two months later in Lisbon on 11 October 2003, Cristiano will be in the starting line-up for the first time against Albania. And gradually, he earns his way into the squad for Euro 2004, which is being held in Portugal. But it's a tournament that will end in tears for the youngster. Lost and alone in the centre of the pitch, he is oblivious to the consolatory words and gestures from his teammates, crying because he never could have imagined losing in the final to Greece. It is just the first of many disappointments with the national team.

Germany World Cup, 2006: 21-year-old Ronaldo has been included by the fans in the list of six young candidates for player of the tournament, alongside Leo Messi and Ecuador's Luis Valencia. But despite the individual recognition, things end in tears once again. Thanks to a Zidane penalty, France knock Portugal out of the running in the semi-final. The Blues go on to play Italy in the final in Berlin – the final of Zidane's headbutt and a fourth World Cup win for Italy. On 8 July, Portugal are defeated 3-1 by Germany in the race for third place at the Gottlieb-Daimler-Stadion in Stuttgart.

Two years later in the Austria-Switzerland Euro 2008 tournament, Germany beat Portugal once again. Joachim Löw's team knock them out 3-2 in the quarter-finals. Despite coming off the best season of his career, winning everything with Man United, Cristiano has failed to shine. He has only scored one goal, against the Czech Republic. To be fair, he has played through a serious ankle injury. 'It was like being stabbed with a knife, I never want to feel pain like that again, it was torturous, both physically and psychologically,' he will later say.

Finally, it is time for the South Africa World Cup. On 13 June 2010, at the first press conference in Magaliesberg, where the Portuguese team are staying, the newly ordained captain seems relaxed, happy and motivated ahead of the upcoming challenge. 'I want to be the best in the tournament. I'm not saying I'll necessarily be the top goal-scorer or anything like that, but I'm going to give it my all and try to be the best. I've come here to play well and help my team win.' It's been fifteen months since Cristiano scored for his country, and he's hoping to remedy that. Portugal make it through the group stage unbeaten and the only team of the 32 World Cup finalists to have kept a completely clean sheet. It's nil-nil against the Ivory Coast, 7-0 against North Korea and nil-nil against Brazil. With five points, Portugal have made it through to the final sixteen after coming second in the group to the Canaries.

In the final sixteen they face Spain, who have come top in Group H. Cristiano has terrorised the Spanish defenders in La Liga, he has won entire games on his own, he's the leader of the Portuguese team and star of the World Cup along with Leo Messi. It's true that with Portugal he hasn't put on quite such a stellar performance, and he hasn't succeeded in showing the fans what he has shown the Spanish crowds during his first year at Real. But against North Korea in South Africa he has broken his scoring curse and netted the sixth of Portugal's seven goals. He is awarded best player in the group phase and is seen as the number one threat in the upcoming match against Spain. In addition, the fans are dying to see how he will fair against his own teammates, Sergio Ramos and Íker Casillas, as well as against Barça defenders Piqué and Puyol, whom he has faced in some historic duels.

On 29 June 2010 at Green Point stadium in Cape Town, the teams sing their national anthems but Cristiano stays silent. It's not a good sign – almost a premonition of what will happen in the match. In short, it's a disaster. Cristiano has just four shots, two on target. The match finishes 1-0 and Spain celebrate the win.

Ronaldo walks away from his defeated and broken team. He is booed by the Spanish fans, and even some of the Portuguese. The camera follows him closely as he heads for the dressing room, his face expressionless. Suddenly he turns and spits – it's unclear whether it's directed at the cameraman or the ground. Either way it's an ugly gesture and the Barcelona press pounce on it, criticising the Real player's behaviour.

His pointed statement after the match also sparks plenty of anger: 'How do I explain Portugal's elimination? Ask Carlos Queiroz.'

Coach Queiroz responds at the press conference: 'While I'm in charge of the national team, if the size of the shirt is too small for anybody they do not need to be here ... Nobody is above the national team and never will be while I'm here.' But when asked if he perhaps should not have given such an important role to Cristiano, he defends his captain: 'That question is out of order. [He] is our leader, our captain. I believe in him.' But former Portugal captain and hero Luís Figo disagrees: 'Regardless of failure or elimination, a captain always has to defend his team. Even if he was the one who took the biggest hit in terms of his reputation. Above all, he should put on a brave face for the team throughout, even in the most difficult moments.'

In an attempt to calm the situation Cristiano puts out an official statement via Jorge Mendes's agency GestiFute. 'I am suffering and I have the right to suffer alone. When I said people should ask the coach [why Portugal were eliminated], it was because he was at the press conference and I didn't feel I was in the right frame of mind to explain things. As the captain I have always taken my responsibilities seriously and will continue to do so, but at that moment I would not have been able to string together more than three or four coherent sentences. I never thought that such a simple comment would provoke such a reaction. Don't go looking for phantoms – you won't find any.'

Unfortunately for Cristiano, his other World Cup phantoms are much more real than the polemic sparked by his comments to the press. The biggest thing haunting the most expensive player in the world – the national team captain, the universal superstar, who has scored a total of 159 goals during his time at Sporting, Man United and Real – is his woeful World Cup balance sheet. In Germany he was shielded from criticism because he was only 21 and Portugal put on such a good performance anyway. But his contributions were one penalty against Iran and one against England. He has played the full length of each of the four matches and he has managed 21 shots on target, but he has only scored one goal. There has been no sign of his usual dazzling self. 'Did the formation limit Cristiano, or was he the one who was unable to give more?' asks Lisbon sports paper *Record* the following day.

The Portuguese fans need Ronaldo to play the way he does in Madrid and score an avalanche of goals – something he has yet to do for his home country. He has scored 32 in 90 international fixtures, an average of 0.36. And in the big matches he has scored just five: a total of three in Euro 2004 and Euro 2008, and one in each of the 2006 and 2010 World Cups. The fans want to see him demonstrate the leadership skills he has honed at Real. They want a Cristiano in the mould of Maradona in the 1986 Mexico World Cup, a captain who can guide his team to the trophy.

The next opportunity to prove that he is the leader of a winning team is Euro 2012. But in the first two matches Cristiano doesn't live up to Portugal's expectations. Against Germany he goes unnoticed. And he has a disastrous night against Denmark. Back in Portugal there is plenty of criticism, and not just about his performance, but about his outbursts, and his conduct on the pitch, such as his criticism of his colleagues when things aren't going well. He is accused of egotism, of thinking too much about himself and not enough about the team.

'He is not mature enough to be the captain, it was irresponsible of Scolari. Now nobody can keep his ego in check,' former Portuguese Football Federation director António Simões tells *Diario de Noticias*. 'And that's detrimental for the team, and for Cristiano himself.' His teammates defend him to the hilt. 'There's nothing wrong with Cristiano,' declares Varela. 'He's our captain and he gives his all to the team every day. He has sacrificed so much for Portugal.'

Everything changes on 17 June against Holland. Cristiano demonstrates his class, destroying the Oranges' defence and sending Portugal through to the quarter-finals with two goals. Four days later, his incredible header beats the outstretched hands of Petr Čech to eliminate the Czech Republic. The following day, the Portuguese press, the world's media, rivals and friends are now ready to weigh in on CR7's talents. 'Best in the world', says the *Record* front page. 'Worth his weight in gold', writes *O Jogo*.

Unfortunately, Portugal will come face to face with Spain once again, in the semi-finals on 27 June in Donetsk. But even after extra time it's still nil-nil. The whistle goes without a single shot on target from Cristiano. He has only managed seven attempts: five misses and two runs that were blocked by the defenders. Time for penalties. Captain Cristiano plans to take the fifth, but he never gets the chance. By then, Cesc Fàbregas has already converted the winning spot-kick to put Spain through to the final. 'So unfair!' he mumbles to the cameras.

It's not a happy ending, but at least this time there is some love for Ronaldo and the Portuguese team. The day after their defeat, they are cheered by hundreds of fans and given a hero's welcome as they arrive at Lisbon airport. 'We wanted to show Ronaldo that he's done well. He's the best player in the world,' says one youngster who has come to the airport with his friends.

CR7 has finally conquered the hearts of the Portuguese. And it won't be long before he delights them again – with an epic hat-trick in Solna against

Sweden on 19 November 2013, helping his country to qualify for the Brazil 2014 World Cup. It's also a personal victory against Ibrahimović, who has scored both of Sweden's goals.

No one in his home country is in any doubt, Cristiano is the best in the world. Even though the Portugal national team are knocked out in the group phases of the World Cup for the first time since 2002, and CR7 only scores a single goal. In his defence, it has to be said that he arrives at the tournament quite worn out after a long and successful season with Real Madrid. There is the usual criticism from the press, but this time the team rallies round him. 'We are leaving with our heads held high. We tried to do our best but football is like this,' says Cristiano when they are eliminated. For the third time, he has been unable to realise his dreams. He has participated in three World Cups, played 1,202 minutes in thirteen matches and scored three goals. At least he can console himself with being Portugal's highest scorer. By the time of the next World Cup, Russia 2018, he will be 33. Who knows …

10 July 2016: the Euro 2016 final. France and Portugal go out onto the pitch at 9pm in Saint-Denis, Paris. The first few minutes pass with neither pain nor glory, but just after the first quarter of an hour Ronaldo gets a tough blow from Dimitri Payet. The referee doesn't see it and play continues. But not

for Cristiano. It quickly becomes apparent that the number 7 is not okay. He's limping, and holding the affected leg. With each run it becomes clear that he is injured, until finally he falls to the ground. The medics bandage his knee on the touchline and he comes back onto the pitch. His team-mates and his entire country can breathe a sigh of relief: it seems to have been just a scare. Ronaldo carries Portugal's hopes of making up for the final they lost against Greece in 2004. With him there, anything seems possible. Which is why, when the Portugal star is on the ground again just a few minutes later, asking to be substituted and unable to contain his tears, it seems as though that's it for Portugal. He comes off in the 24th minute, removing his captain's armband and crying inconsolably. Welshman Gareth Bale, CR7's team-mate at Real Madrid, takes to Twitter to voice what many are thinking: 'Terrible to see Cris come off like that. Hope it's nothing too bad.'

Without the number 7, 90 minutes pass without any goals. It's the same story in the first half of extra time, before Éderzito António Macedo Lopes, aka Éder, becomes the hero of the match, making it 1-0 in the 108th minute and unleashing a collective euphoria. A bandaged Ronaldo, still limping, is on his feet following the last few moments of the match from the touchline, shouting instructions to his team-mates. When the final whistle goes, the Madeiran goes back onto

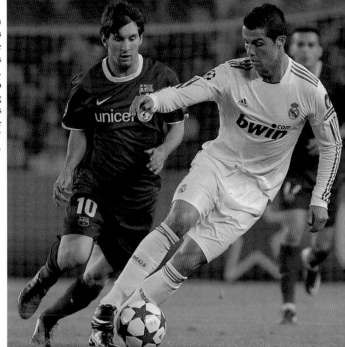

(right) Action from Barcelona versus Real Madrid in the 2011 Champions League semi-final. Messi and Ronaldo have been battling it out in Spain's *El Clásico* since 2009 ... (AP Photo/ Andres Kudacki)

(below) ... and in 2013 Neymar joined them. In his first *Clásico* he scored one goal and set up another as Barça won the game 2-1. (AP Photo/Emilio Morenatti)

The trio have found major international trophies hard to come by but Brazil's 2013 Confederations Cup win hinted at a bright future for Neymar and the *Seleção*. (AP Photo/Victor Caivano)

Ronaldo's heroics in World Cup qualifying ensured that Portugal would join Neymar's Brazil and Messi's Argentina in the final tournament. Against Sweden in a play-off, the number 7 scored all four of his team's goals in a 4-2 aggregate win. (Getty Images)

Meanwhile, Messi continues to make history. His two goals against Rayo Vallecano in February 2014 made him the third highest goalscorer in La Liga history. 'He can break any record he sets his mind to,' commented Barcelona coach Tata Martino. (Getty Images)

Ronaldo with his partner Irina and son Cristiano Junior at the FIFA Ballon d'Or gala in January 2014. (Bongarts/Getty Images)

Proud father Messi with Antonella and his son Thiago. In the background, Neymar is also introducing David Lucca to the crowd at Nou Camp. (Getty Images)

the pitch for the third time, but this time it's to celebrate. And shed more tears. He has finally achieved his greatest dream: winning a title with his national team.

* * *

Lionel Messi has said on various occasions that his biggest ambition is to be world champion with the Albiceleste – the 'white and sky blues', as Argentina are known. After winning every possible award and title at both an individual and club level, Leo needs to win one with his national team in order to conquer once and for all the Argentine fans, who have taken time to warm to him. Leo's international journey hasn't exactly been a bed of roses.

Let's look back to the 2006 World Cup in Germany. Thanks to Leo's success in the Under 20 World Cup in Holland, coach José Pekerman has included him in his 23-strong squad. The Argentines have pinned all their hopes on him; they want to see confirmation of all the amazing stories that are told across Europe about Maradona's heir. Since the days of the 'Pibe de Oro' (Golden Boy – Maradona's nickname) they have dreamt there would be another player, a spectacular, magical player, whom they could love and worship the way they did, and still do, with Diego. Both multinational and Argentine companies have bet on Leo in order to benefit from the effects of a global stage. But he is still only eighteen years old, and it should be remembered that no Argentine has played in the final stages of a World Cup at that age. Maradona wasn't even selected by César Luis Menotti for the 1978 World Cup.

In the first match against the Ivory Coast, Leo is on the bench, after Pekerman weighs up not only his age but a recent injury. He has recovered, but his muscle still seems to be bothering him. Against Serbia and Montenegro at the Gelsenkirchen stadium on 16 June he is on the bench once again. But this time, he gets to make his World Cup debut when he comes on for Maxi Rodriguez in the 74th minute. In the 87th minute, Tévez passes to Crespo, who passes back to Tévez who sends it down to Messi, who is motoring up the right wing. He gets past the defender and scores the sixth goal, sliding the ball between the post and the goalkeeper's hand. Then he pauses to point to the player who gifted him the goal. Crespo rushes over to hug him, the crowd goes wild. This makes up for his unfortunate 2005 debut.

And for the final Group C match against Holland, with both teams already through to the final sixteen, Pekerman is happy enough to put him in the starting line-up. Expectation is mounting in the stands. What wonders will Lionel have for them this time? If he wreaked havoc in fifteen minutes, who knows what he will do in 90. And even if this isn't his night, the effect of his presence on the pitch is almost palpable.

On 24 June, his nineteenth birthday, Messi is back to being a spectator for 84 long minutes against Mexico. When he finally comes on for Saviola, the score is 1-1. The game is heading into extra time. And it is then that the boy from Barça changes the team's rhythm, sending the ball from foot to foot, building up to an amazing Maxi Rodríguez goal. Argentina have scraped through into the quarter-finals.

In Berlin, on 30 June, they face host team Germany. There are 120 minutes of play, but Leo Messi does not play even a single minute. It is a mystery, the talking point of a match that ends with Argentina losing on penalties (4-2, after a 1-1 scoreline at the end of extra time). Why didn't Pekerman bring him on? Popular consensus seems to be that if he had come on, Argentina would have sealed the match before it got to the penalty shoot-out stage. He would have taken charge of transforming the situation. 'People were expecting Messi to be the great Maradona of this World Cup. And he was just taking his first steps with Argentina, a great team. I hope this experience will serve him well in the future,' Pekerman will later say. As for Leo, he acknowledges: 'Pekerman decided that was the way it was going to be. He had players like Saviola and Crespo who had been doing really well, and that's that.'

Fast forward four years to South Africa, and now it's Diego Armando Maradona himself at the helm.

The 'Pelusa', as Diego is also known, has been indulging his protégé, and on the eve of the tournament he says: 'I think Leo is the best in the world. And he's Argentine. I've already told the boys: 'If he gets the ball, we'll have plenty of chances.' I'm trying to get it into their heads that they're a team. And that we need Messi to play the way he does at Barça. Messi knows that his teammates want him to be the cherry on the cake. He needs to lead them.'

On Saturday 12 June at Johannesburg's Ellis Park, Messi lives up to all the attention and compliments, and shows himself to be the best in Argentina. At the end of the match, won by a header from Gabriel Heinze, Maradona rushes over to Messi and lifts him up in his arms. He squeezes him tight against his Tarantino-worthy suit and tie, and kisses him energetically. Leo later acknowledges their relationship: 'In the national team I hadn't been myself. I wasn't playing the way I was at Barcelona, and it was noticeable. But I always had Diego's support and everything changed thanks to my teammates' belief in me. I would love for everyone in Argentina to feel about me the way they do in Barcelona.' It seems that Leo is finally winning over the fans, who at first were distant towards the only player in the squad who had never played at a senior level in an Argentine club. Plus, he has never been at his Barcelona best with the Albiceleste. And up until now, he hasn't been a leader, a commander-in-chief – in other words, he hasn't been the new Maradona.

In the final group match against Greece, the Pelusa has a big surprise in store for his number 10. He will be wearing the captain's armband for the first time. It's the recognition everyone has been waiting for. After a tough match hampered by the cold, Argentina win 2-0 and claim their place in the last sixteen with three group-stage victories. They have gone from outside chance to favourites for the trophy.

On 27 June the Albiceleste beat Javier Aguirre's Mexico 3-1 in the final sixteen match with minimal effort, although Messi doesn't score. 'I have to score two against Germany or that's it,' jokes the number 10 at the end of the match. But it's not to be. In the quarter-finals, Schweinsteiger, Müeller, Özil, Khedira and Cross are too much for the Argentines. Maradona's tactical gamble, which had been hailed as revolutionary, fails Messi again and again, just when it matters most. Stuck far away from the goal, Lionel loses the ball twelve times and doesn't manage to get it back. He is despairing at the fact that on the few occasions when he does manage to break free from the Germans, his teammates don't manage to feed him the ball. He is left in no man's land, foundering fast.

His World Cup score sheet is dismal. He has played five matches, he has taken more shots than anyone

– 30 times, twelve on target and two off the post – but he hasn't scored a single goal. The following day, the headlines in the Argentine press tell the story:

'World Cup humiliation for the national team.
   The worst fall since 1974'   *Clarín*
'Germany crushes Argentina'   *La Nación*
'No goals or glory for Messi'   *Olé*
'Tears for Messi and Argentina'   *Perfil*

After the match, Messi stays silent. But Maradona admits it has been 'the hardest moment in my life, a real blow'. A few days later, a few lines appear on a Mandarin blog called Tencent, allegedly quoting Messi, although it's not confirmed: 'I feel really awful, I want to go home. We played badly, we failed to live up to everyone's expectations, and now we have to start all over again.'

Starting all over again also involves a new coach, Sergio 'el Checho' Batista, and the next challenge is the 2011 Copa América. But it's another thwarted dream, another 'national failure', reports *Olé*. On 16 June 2011, Argentina are knocked out by Uruguay in a penalty shoot-out on their home turf, in what was supposed to be 'their' cup. And just as in the World Cup, Leo Messi is going home without having scored a single goal. *Olé* likens it to the 2007 Copa América, when, under Alfio 'el Coco' Basile, Argentina were beaten 3-0 by Brazil in the final. And there was plenty of criticism directed towards Messi on that occasion too. 'He did very little to try to change the outcome,' wrote *Clarín*. 'He was blocked by the Brazilian defence and remained trapped in his labyrinth.'

Leo has suffered plenty of disappointment with the Albiceleste. The only bright spot is during the 2008 Olympic Games in Beijing, where Argentina quash and humiliate Brazil. Agüero, with two goals and a hand in the third (he is fouled and Riquelme converts the penalty), are all evidence of the weakness of Dunga's team and Ronaldinho's decline. Without making a big impression, Leo has won that highly anticipated duel with his friend, mentor and former teammate Ronnie. He is happy. Ronnie only wants to hide, to disappear from the face of the earth. 'I'm sad, very sad,' he will say later. Leo is there to console him, but then it's time to move on towards that coveted gold.

On 23 August 2008 at the Beijing National Stadium, nicknamed the Bird's Nest, the Albiceleste beat Nigeria in the final thanks to a goal from Ángel Di María, the ex-Rosario Central player, now at Real Madrid. Messi and Kun Agüero rush over to embrace each other, celebrating their gold medal success – and, finally, a dream come true.

But of course, the Flea still dreams of winning a World Cup. When he lands in Brazil in the summer of 2014 he is convinced this is his big chance. He is now the lynchpin in Alejandro Sabella's line-up, the captain and clear leader. And everything appears to be going well, he seems to be on the verge of fulfilling his greatest dream … but then luck deserts him. On 13 July at the Maracanã stadium in Rio de Janeiro, Lionel feels like a world champion for nearly 120 minutes. But Germany brings him back down to earth with a bump thanks to a Mario Götze goal – just when everyone thought the match was heading into penalties. Germany have done it again.

The Mannschaft are longstanding rivals of the Argentines, and they certainly know how to crush their dreams. They did it in humiliating fashion in the quarter-finals in South Africa in 2010, and they did it with penalties on their home turf in 2006. Leo had one mission: to lead the national team to triumph just as Maradona did in his day. Even the Pelusa himself has named Leo as his successor. But they are separated by almost 30 years, and an enormous imbalance in terms of luck. 'It's been a long time since Argentina made it past the quarter-final. At last we were in the final,' he explains after leaving the dressing room, after the defeat has begun to sink in. 'We will always carry the disappointment of not being able to seal the deal. We were so close. Losing in the last few moments of extra time is gutting, but I think we can leave with our heads held high.'

The Rosarino is leaving Brazil with the Golden Ball for player of the tournament, but there is plenty of controversy surrounding the award. Some feel that the thirteen wise men of FIFA entrusted with making the decision have opted for publicity over quality. One such person is Maradona himself: 'I would give Leo the moon, but when the marketing gurus want him to win something he didn't win, it's not fair.' And Leo confirms that he has no interest in the prize: 'I don't care about the Golden Ball, I wanted to lift the World Cup.'

Aside from that, Leo can console himself with having been decisive for his team during the first four matches, although his performance went somewhat downhill after that. He has scored four goals in total, two fewer than the tournament's top goal-scorer, Colombia's James Rodríguez.

A year later, at the Copa América, the Albiceleste stumble once again in the final, against host nation Chile on 4 July 2015 at the Estadio Nacional in Santiago. This time the match goes to penalties. Leo doesn't miss but his team-mates Gonzálo Higuaín and Éver Banega do.

And the curse of Messi and Argentina continues the following year on 26 June 2016 in the final of the Centenary Copa América at the MetLife stadium in East Rutherford, New Jersey. Chile win it 4-2 on penalties after a rough and goal-less 120 minutes, lifting their second Copa América trophy in two years. Leo, who has had a great tournament, misses from the penalty spot, before giving way to tears. It's the fourth final – and the third consecutive one – in which the Barça star has fallen from grace with his national team, and he can't contain himself. It's déjà vu, he's in a vicious cycle with the Albiceleste.

It's all too much, and after the match, in the press area, he announces that he will be retiring from international football. 'This is a difficult moment, it's hard to analyse it. In the dressing room I felt that that was it, it was over for me with the national team. That's how I feel right now. I missed an incredibly crucial penalty. I have done everything I could, I have fought on many occasions and tried many times to be a champion with Argentina. It's been four finals and I couldn't win them. It's a great sadness that it keeps happening. It hurts me more than anything, but it's clear that it's not meant to be for me. I wanted more than anything to win a title with my country and unfortunately it didn't happen, I couldn't do it. That's it, it's better for everyone this way.'

Immediately, the hashtag #NotevayasLeo – 'Don't go Leo' – goes viral. In his home country, no one has lost hope that the top scorer in the history of the Albiceleste will change his mind and come back to guide his team. And on 12 August 2016 that hope is realised when Messi confirms at a press conference that he is thinking of continuing with international football, backtracking on the idea of leaving the Albiceleste. 'I love my country and my national shirt too much. I see that there are problems with Argentine football and I don't want to create another one. I am grateful to everyone who wants me to continue playing with Argentina, and I hope that we can bring you some joy soon,' concludes the Flea.

* * *

Speaking of failures … Neymar's first big disappointment with his national team occurs at the London 2012 Olympic Games. During the first five matches of the competition the Brazilian has been upstoppable. He has scored three goals and made four assists, and is the second-highest goal-scorer in the team after Leandro Damião, who has netted six. Neymar has been satisfied with his performance up until now, although he has refrained from focusing on it, insisting that his role is the same as everyone else's – helping Brazil conquer the final frontier. The most decorated national football team in the world has yet to win an Olympic gold medal. Ronaldo, Rivaldo, Bebeto and Ronaldinho have all had a go, without success. This time around it seemed like the Canaries had a real opportunity, but it isn't to be. On 11 August 2012, Mexico takes the gold, knocking Brazil out of their third Olympic final, following defeats in 1984 by France and 1988 at the hands of the Soviet Union. While the Mexicans celebrate, Neymar cries inconsolably on Wembley's hallowed turf.

The following day, the Brazilian press are full of negative talk about Juninho's performance. They claim it is his second failure, after the 2011 Copa América in which Brazil lost to Paraguay on penalties in the quarter-finals. There are some who are even in doubt as to the number 11's place in the squad for the Brazil World Cup. His international career, which began in an explosive way, seems to have come to a standstill.

Criticism from both the media and the fans intensifies in 2013. Neymar has been through a difficult patch with Brazil – he hasn't managed to score the way he usually does at Santos. Some allege he has been more concerned about his hairstyle, advertising commitments and Barcelona transfer talks than the national team. But in the Confederations Cup on 15 June 2013 in Brasilia, wearing the number 10 in a match against Japan, Neymar proves them all wrong with a spectacular goal. Marcelo crosses from the left, Fred controls it on his chest and, with the ball still in the air, Neymar connects with his right foot, sending the ball flying into the top corner of the net at 98 kilometres an hour. The shot will later make it onto the shortlist for FIFA's Puskás Award, which rewards the best goal of the year.

On 19 June, before the second match, Neymar shows his support for public protests taking place across Brazil, writing on his Facebook page: 'I'm sad about everything that's happening in Brazil. I have always hoped it would never get to the point where people would need to take to the streets to demand better transport, healthcare, education and security. It is the government's DUTY to provide this. My parents have worked very hard to give me and my sister the basics in life. Today, thanks to the success with which you honour me, this might sound demagogic, but it isn't. Let's wave our flags in favour of the protests that are happening across Brazil. I'm BRAZILIAN and I love my country! I have family and friends who live in Brazil. I, too, want a more just, safe, healthy and HONEST Brazil! The only way I can represent and defend Brazil is by playing football. But, starting from this match against Mexico, I will go out onto the pitch inspired by this incredible public protest.'

There is no doubt he is inspired. He shines not only against Mexico, but against Italy and then Uruguay, carrying Brazil to the final in Rio de Janeiro. It's the final everyone was hoping for: Brazil versus Spain, the current world and European champions. In the 44th minute, Oscar and Neymar go on an explosive counter-attack. Oscar has the ball just outside the area and Neymar holds back to avoid being caught offside, waiting for his teammate to pass it to him. He receives it just on the edge of the box, prepares to shoot, and unleashes a cannon with his left foot that slams into the net just under Íker Casillas's crossbar. It's a sensational goal, and the number 10 celebrates with the fans in the stands. It's his fourth goal in the tournament, and it brings the world champions to their knees. It's 3-0 to Brazil at the final whistle, and the Maracanã stadium erupts into a fiesta. And Neymar gets to pose with three trophies: the Confederations Cup, the Golden Ball for best player, and the Bronze Boot for the third-highest goal-scorer of the tournament.

It's a world away from the images captured by the world's media just twelve months later. For Ney, Friday 4 July 2014 will be remembered as one of the worst days of his life. Everything is going well, his team have already done enough to go through to the semis of the World Cup, when Colombian defender Juan Camilo Zúñiga knees him in the back. Ney falls face down on the ground, screaming in pain, holding his back. Marcelo runs over to him and the Barça forward tells him he can't feel his legs. The whole team fear the worst. His pain is all too visible as he is rushed off on a stretcher. A few hours later the doctors confirm the fracture in his third vertebra, an incredibly rare injury in football that will keep him out for three to six weeks. Neymar's World Cup is over. 'If he had hit me two centimetres closer to the middle, I could be in a wheelchair,' he tells the press a few days later.

'It is difficult to talk about something that happened at such an important juncture in my career,' he adds, trying to remain calm. He bows his head and wipes away tears in silence.

His pain is that of a nation who dreamt of bringing home their sixth World Cup, after triumphs in Sweden in 1958, Chile in 1962, Mexico in 1970, the United States in 1994 and Japan and South Korea in 2002. But four days after his injury, the team endure a crushing defeat at the hands of Germany. Ney is watching at home with family and friends. No one thought the match against the favourites would be easy, and it was clear that the Canaries would be weak without Neymar. But absolutely no one was expecting a more painful and humiliating 'Maracanazo' than the original. It ends 1-7, but Neymar has already switched off by then. According to Brazilian website UOL Esporte, frustrated with events in Belo Horizonte, he shouts: 'Screw it, I don't want to see any more of this shit. Let's play poker!'

With the memory of that particular disaster still fresh, Ney goes out onto the pitch in La Serena, Chile, on 14 June 2015 to play the first match of the Copa América against Peru. The Brazilians have pinned all their hopes on the magic of the young *Blaugrana* player, and the pundits are in no doubt that he is a cut above the rest of his team-mates. He heads their first goal in the fifth minute, a crucial shot that rallies the team after they had already conceded a goal by Christian Cueva in the first few touches of the game. With Brazil having little more in the way of tactics than passing to the Barça number 11, it all rests on Ney. And he doesn't disappoint: he scores, he makes nineteen attempts (more than in the entire previous tournament in 2011), he manages six shots on target, he dazzles with a double 'sombrero' – two flicks over the heads of two opponents with consecutive touches – and finally he sets up Douglas Costa's winning goal in injury time. It's an agonising victory, but Ney makes it possible.

At the age of 23 he is the youngest player to have scored 44 goals for Brazil, and in the list of historic goal-scorers he is up there behind only Pelé, Ronaldo, Zico and Romario. He is a symbol of hope for his country, a warm and charismatic kid, although he occasionally lets his emotions get the better of him. Like on 18 June in a clash with Colombia, which ends in a 0-1 defeat for Brazil and is to be his last match of the tournament. He isn't out injured like in the World Cup, this time he is sidelined due to an unjustified outburst. When the final whistle goes Ney kicks the ball, hitting Pablo Armero in the back. Is it bad luck, or a deliberate strike? A general brawl ensues between the two sides, and Chilean referee Enrique Osses pulls out his red card.

But the Barça number 11's outburst isn't over. He

later squares up to the referee in the tunnel, hurling insults at him. 'You were trying to make a name for yourself at my expense,' he allegedly says, according to the referee's official match report. He is immediately banned for four matches by the Disciplinary Tribunal of CONMEBOL – the South American Football Federation. There is plenty of criticism, including from his fellow Brazilians. 'He is behaving in a very aggressive way and that's not acceptable,' says Ronaldo Nazário da Lima. Brazil coach Dunga seems to be in agreement: 'We need men who can make decisions, even if they get it wrong; we don't need children.' The rest of the squad follows Ney home just a week later, after a defeat by Paraguay on penalties in the quarter-finals.

A year later, Neymar misses the Centennial Copa América due to a decision taken by Barça. 'FC Barcelona thanks the Brazilian Football Federation and its president, Marco Polo del Nero, who has accepted the club's request for Neymar to play in the 2016 Olympic Games in Brazil, which will be held between 3rd and 21st August. For this reason, Neymar Júnior has been excused from playing in the Copa América which will be held in the United States between 3rd and 26th June,' explains the club in a press release. Without the pressure of the tournament in the States, Ney can concentrate on the Olympics in his home country. And his efforts pay off. On

20th August, the Canaries and their star break the curse to beat Germany in the final. The Brazilians go ahead in the 27th minute with a goal by Ney from a dead ball. During the next half hour things look to be heading in their favour, when the Mannschaft equalise and threaten yet another Greek tragedy. The scoreline remains the same during extra time, and it all comes down to penalties. In the fifth round, Germany's Nils Petersen misses … and Neymar heads straight up to the penalty spot. He knows it's all resting on him, if he scores, the gold is his. And he doesn't disappoint. The entire Maracaná crowd leaps to its feet, while the star cannot contain his emotion. He is the Olympic champion, and thanks to him the Canaries can put one of the saddest periods in their history firmly behind them.

Chapter 7
Style and abilities

A straight line, a zigzag, a curve. Sometimes a single geometric term is enough to describe someone's game.

As Spanish writer Manuel Vicent points out: 'Cristiano Ronaldo subscribes to the Euclid school of thought: that a straight line is the shortest distance between two points. He generally makes a rapid beeline for the goal.' Lionel Messi on the other hand, takes more of a meandering, angular route across the pitch, while Neymar favours a curved trajectory. 'Following a curve rather than running directly towards goal is one way to create improvised space out wide,' says José Miguel Wisnik, Brazilian musician, composer and writer. 'It's as much a way of penetrating the opponent's space as it is aesthetically pleasing.'

Speaking of aesthetics, renowned Brazilian ex-footballer Eduardo Gonçalves de Andrade, better known as 'Tostão', defines Neymar's style as 'Baroque', while Messi's is 'minimalist'. He explains: 'Lionel does very few tricks, only those that are absolutely necessary to do something extraordinary. Neymar is more theatrical, more showy – he's always looking to provide spectacle, enjoy himself while demonstrating his abilities with the ball.' In fact, Tostão compares Messi to Pelé and Neymar to Maradona: 'Like Leo, O Rei has an incredible capacity for synthesis, which Neymar lacks. Pelé can always find a way to score with the fewest possible movements. I've never seen him take an unnecessary step. He used to dodge around his opponents with the sole purpose of getting to the goal, just like Messi. He played a tidy game. Maradona, on the other hand, loved to show off his abilities.'

Although in truth, Neymar's style has evolved since he arrived at Barcelona. He has matured as a player, and has adapted to the club's signature strategy just as other greats who came before him, like Zlatan Ibrahimović. But in contrast to the Swede, Ney found his place from the moment he arrived. He went from being the spoiled kid at Santos to being Messi's perfect apprentice, and when the Argentine was injured at the start of the 2015–16 season he became the team's driving force alongside Luis Suárez. He continues to unsettle the opponent's defensive line, letting his individualism and his penchant for elaborate tricks shine through from time to ¬time, but he now has a capacity for self-sacrifice that was unheard of in the past.

And what's Cristiano's style? With his constant

search for perfection, he fits the 'classical' mould. He has constantly refined his play, eliminating even the tiniest flourishes to perfect the most utilitarian form and winning formula. Both he and Messi are products of their footballing experience: CR7 started out at a Portuguese academy before moving through the rigorous training of British football. Messi, on the one hand, has Argentine flair, but also demonstrates his deeply Barcelonian style of play. Meanwhile Neymar embodies the most recent example of the great Brazilian tradition of what Italian film director, writer and football fan Pier Paolo Pasolini defined, in a 1971 essay, as 'footballing poetry', rather than the practical 'prose' of European football. Neymar is the artist, Messi is the magician, while Cristiano is force times technique.

But all three share an innate ability, a sort of sixth sense – something that could be likened to that of Canadian ice hockey player Wayne Gretzky, often hailed as the greatest hockey player of all time. When asked to reveal his secret, Gretzky has been known to say: 'It's simple; I skate to where the puck is going, not where it's been.' In the words of Neymar's first coach, Betinho: 'Neymar could always see what was going to happen before everyone else could. He was always a step ahead. He knew where the ball was going and how his opponent would react.' This capacity for anticipating the opponent's movements and intercepting their attempts at goal is a fundamental factor in making or breaking a game – and all three do it in their own special style.

Leo Messi has impressive control – the ball always seems to be glued to his left foot. He moves well in small spaces, with or without the ball, and he can turn in the tightest spots imaginable – it's impossible to tell which way he will go. He's one of those rare players who can control the ball without looking at it. That allows him to watch the opposition and his team-mates, and make an unprecedented pass. He can do it because he sees the whole pitch. In addition, Messi has 'physical thinking'. He is mind and body all at the same time. He has the same gift that Pelé, Maradona and Di Stéfano had. It's the speed with which his brain tells his legs what to do. Messi gets an idea and, bam! it's already happened.

In fact, Dutch medical researcher Pieter Medendorp of Radboud University in Nijmegen has studied Messi's brain to try to understand how he makes decisions. 'Messi makes a decision to run, jump or shoot in a fraction of a second, and we want to figure out how this happens in his head,' explains Medendorp. 'What triggers him opting for one course or another? On the pitch he knows exactly where everyone else is, and in that moment he decides not only how to dodge a defender or where to go, but also which foot to use and what to do with the ball.'

Physical thinking aside, a lot has to do with speed. Messi is still incredibly accurate even at maximum velocity – no mean feat, as high speed often leads to collisions. He can burst into a run, accelerate, dribble in and out, turn, assist or score, and invent something new in an instant – and all the while looking for support and doing one-twos, playing for the team. His impressive teamwork is something he has developed over time – at school he was more of an individual, the kid that had that 'give me the ball, I want to play, I want to enjoy myself', vibe.

Little Cristiano was similar – and sometimes it still shows on the pitch when he clamours or gestures for the ball, itching to seal the deal in a match. He has undoubtedly evolved and matured since his first seasons at Man United. He plays well with his teammates, gets more involved in defensive situations, and knows how to read the flow of the match. But his individual characteristics have not changed – rather, they have intensified. He is even more physically fit, has the muscular make-up of an elite athlete, speed to rival that of Usain Bolt, accuracy with either foot and, above all, a powerful kick that practically slices through the ball, particularly when taking free kicks. In addition, his arching shots can be extremely complicated for a goalie. He's a superb goal-scorer, fierce and hungry, always trying to improve, always trying to ignite the next fight. 'For Cristiano there are no victories or lasting defeats, everything starts again after a match,' says Aurélio Pereira. 'He's 50 per cent mental focus and 50 per cent passion for training, football and professionalism.'

Former player and Argentine coach Jorge Valdano analyses the evolution of Messi and CR7: 'It's incredible that they have modified their style of play in opposite directions. Cristiano has moved forward 20 yards, while Messi has found his best form by moving back 20 yards. It seems natural that Cristiano would maintain his goal-scoring prowess by moving closer to the goal, but it seems counterintuitive that Messi would achieve the same by retreating from it.' Sources close to Real have dared to speculate on the Portuguese's future position on the pitch, given his manoeuvrability: 'He's tall, strong, heads the ball well, shoots with both feet … he has the makings of a centre forward,' they tell *Marca*. A position the Real star has always disliked, 'because it means having his back to the goal. He prefers to be on the wing so that he has it in his sights,' explains Carlo Ancelotti, one of the coaches who knows CR7 best.

The Barça camp also has alternative plans for Messi, but curiously, they involve the polar opposite approach. He would remain the lynchpin of the *Blaugrana* attacking line-up, enjoying full freedom of movement, but would keep the physical wear and tear to an absolute minimum. The club wants him to avoid exerting himself unnecessarily, cutting back on the 30 or 40-yard solo slaloms the Flea has become known for over the years, but which are taking their toll on his fitness with every passing year.

Meanwhile, former Santos coach Muricy Ramalho has no doubt about Neymar's greatest virtue: 'His capacity to do things is beyond anyone's imagination. That's exactly what being a superstar boils down to: unexpected plays, improvisation, ingenuity. When everyone thinks he's going one way, he'll go the other, that's why Neymar plays such a crucial role in a match. The defender is convinced he's going to try to go round him on the left, and then he'll chip it. He breaks the rules, and he gets out of situations no one else would manage to get out of.'

Wisnik agrees: 'Neymar has an incredible repertoire, he's surprising and inventive. He'll always come out with something unexpected. Plus he sees the big picture. He makes confident passes and always follows through to the finish – he's not just a dribbler. His style is technically accomplished – elaborate, yes, but devastating.' And on that point, he has begun to be compared with another Brazilian star who defined an era and used to play at Barça: Ronaldinho. Even the club's coach, Luis Enrique, who played with Ronnie before he coached Neymar, acknowledges the parallels: 'When I played with Ronnie we used to stay to watch him doing tricks with the ball during the warm-up, and it's the same with Ney.' There's no doubt as far as Ronaldinho himself is concerned: 'Neymar is already my successor. He's been practising for the role and he'll do it for many years. He's a great player and he will be the face of Brazil in the coming seasons.'

Finally, let's not forget the joy of the game, something for which all three players share a deep appreciation. It's a fundamental aspect of being a champion because, without that passion, that obsession and love of the sport, without that childlike excitement at the opportunity to kick a ball around, even professional football can become boring.

Chapter 8

Secrets of success

'When my brother was five or six years old there was no other present that could make him as happy as a football could,' says Leo Messi's brother Rodrigo. 'He was crazy about football like all kids are. Everyone wants to be a footballer when they're a kid. But he knew how to stay faithful to his childhood passion and pursue his dream because his happiness was, and still is, tied up with football. I was a striker, but Leo had something I never had: he was so strong-willed, he has worked so hard and has made so many sacrifices to become who he is today.'

'Cristiano's life is an example of persistence and hard work – all children who dream of being sportsmen and women need to understand that,' Jorge Mendes tells Spanish newspaper *ABC*. The man who has been Ronaldo's agent since he was sixteen years old adds: 'He gets up early and goes to training. Then he eats. He has to maintain a healthy, balanced diet to be able to put in that level of hard work. In the afternoon he spends some time with Cristiano Junior and takes his afternoon siesta at the same time as him. Then he puts in some time in the pool, usually an hour or two. He is always exercising and taking care of himself. After a light dinner he goes to bed promptly at 11pm. He is the consummate professional – no one is more disciplined. There are others who work just as hard, but no one can top his dedication. His level of passion, commitment and self-sacrifice are admirable. He is never complacent – he always wants more, wants to achieve more. He's not the kind of person who thinks: "I've done really well, and that's good enough." No – he trains every day to be a better footballer.'

'Juninho always loved to play, and has always loved being the best,' recalls Reginaldo 'Fino' Ferreira de Oliveira, Neymar's manager at Portuguesa Santista, who also coached him in indoor football – a highly popular sport in Brazil, known as *futsal*. 'He was the best in the street, the neighbourhood, the town, then the state, then the country, and now he wants to be the best in the world. He is improving every day – it has been that way since he was little.'

In just a few words, Rodrigo Messi, Jorge Mendes and Fino offer an insight into the qualities – talent aside – that are vital to success, the key to the three players' achievements.

The first is commitment to an early passion: Leo, Cristiano and Neymar all loved football from a young age, but what separated them from the other millions of children like them was their persistence in pursuing their dream of becoming a professional. This required a huge amount of commitment and sacrifice – such as moving to Spain in the case of the Messi family. For Cristiano it meant a difficult first few years in Lisbon and then being away from his family when his father died.

And they have sacrificed the chance to have a 'normal' childhood to dedicate themselves to training and matches. 'As a mother, I hope to God he will be happy and that he lives life – because Leo still hasn't really lived,' Celia Cuccittini has said in the past. 'He has dedicated himself body and soul to football. He hasn't been able to do a lot of the things that young people his age do.'

Then there is the hard work. 'To be successful you have to work harder than everyone else,' Cristiano told fellow Real signing Karim Benzema in 2009. But CR7's advice no doubt also applied to himself – former Man United manager Sir Alex Ferguson has described him as the most talented and hardworking footballer he has ever trained. And he's not the only coach to acknowledge Ronaldo's abilities. Former Real manager Carlo Ancelotti has been impressed by his constant capacity to push himself harder. He is one of the first to arrive at the Valdebebas training ground each day, and it's rare for him not to stay behind afterwards to perfect some aspect of his game. The same applies when recovering after a match – he's in the gym, seeing the physio, having contrast hydrotherapy or cryosauna sessions, or doing lengths in the pool, all in an attempt to maintain his fitness and avoid injuries. But it's nothing new: as a kid at the Sporting youth academy the coaches used to find him in the gym at 1am lifting weights without permission. He would do press-ups and sit-ups in the dorm and train with weights around his ankles to improve his dribbling. When his teammates would head for the showers after training sessions, he would stay on the pitch, practising free kicks against a wall of life-sized targets.

Alcides Magri Júnior, Neymar's old futsal coach at Gremetal, has similar memories: 'I remember when we finished training sessions, one of the coaching staff, Edy, would say to Neymar, "Hey kid, come and eat with everyone else." But he paid no attention and kept on playing on his own.' It takes hard work to fulfil childhood dreams, keep learning, improving and progressing, become the best in the neighbourhood, the team and the world – and then stay there. As Roger Federer says in an advert, being the best doesn't end with success, you have to go out there and prove it again and again.

Staying at one's peak takes a sense of professionalism, keeping a level head and treating one's body well. Ronaldo, for example, doesn't smoke or drink, and continues to maintain his strict diet. Players can also find it easier to stay on the straight and narrow if they surround themselves with family and good friends – people who provide a counterpoint to the ever-adoring, admiring fans, and help them keep their feet firmly on the ground. Cristiano has said countless times that his family have been a pillar of strength throughout his life. And Neymar notes: 'I can't predict the future, but I know that my family will always be around me.'

But there is one more thing that marks out the champions from the average sportsmen and women: a thirst for victory, the desire to win, always, whatever the weather, whoever the opponent, whatever the stakes. 'Ronaldo was decisive in everything he did,' recalls Leonel Pontes, his tutor at the Sporting academy. 'He wanted to be the best at everything: table-tennis, tennis, pool, table-football, darts, athletics – even in a one-on-one test of speed. His team always had to win. And he had to win regardless of the sport. I think that's one of the things that has got him to where he is today.' It's that same impulse and determination that has pushed all three players to the top of their game.

Chapter 9

Partners

French symbolist painter Odilon Redon spent 30 years painting his wife, Camille. In 1869 he wrote: 'It is possible to get a sense of a man through his wife or partner. One can understand a man better because of that which the woman loves about him, which, in turn, helps one to get a sense of her. It is rare for an observer not to notice myriad sweet and intimate connections between them.'

One only has to consider the women who, at some time or another, have captured the hearts of these three superstars to see how different they are, even when it comes to love.

Leo Messi has never forgotten his Argentine roots, despite the fact that he has spent more time living in Spain than in his native country. So it's hardly surprising that his partner is Argentine, and, what's more, someone he has known since he was little: Antonella Roccuzzo.

'Time passes, the feelings stay the same ♥ #babies #love,' writes Antonella on her Instagram account, under a black and white photo of her and Leo Messi when they were young. They have known each other since they were five: Antonella is the first cousin of Leo's childhood friend Lucas Scaglia. 'We have seen each other grow up. Our families know each other, so I had no doubts,' the Barça number 10 has said. A Rosario native, a Newell's fan, little like Leo and the same age as him, Antonella is the daughter of Patricia Blanco and José Roccuzzo, a supermarket owner and president of the Rosario supermarket owners' association. She is the second of three sisters, between Paula and Carla, and she studied dentistry and then communications before going to live in Barcelona with Leo.

She says their romance began as early as primary school, and that Leo wrote her a love letter saying that one day she would be his girlfriend. But the little Casanova left for Barcelona soon afterwards, and they didn't see each other again until 2007, when Messi returned to his hometown on one of his visits. They began dating but kept their relationship secret until Leo revealed the romance on 25 January 2009 on Catalan TV3 programme *Hat-trik*. 'Do you have a girlfriend?' one of the kids in the audience asks him on camera. 'I have a girlfriend and she's in Argentina,' Leo replies. 'In fact, everything is going well, I'm very calm about it.'

A few weeks later, on 22 February, he is seen walking through the streets of Sitges with his arm around a girl with long dark hair. The tabloid hunt is on to reveal the identity of the lucky brunette who appears to have conquered the footballer's heart. In May, Leo tells Buenos Aires newspaper *Clarín* that he has been in a relationship for a year. He has managed to keep it under wraps 'because I'm discreet', he says. 'If we hadn't been walking through Sitges during carnival season, no one would even have known,' he adds. But now it's out there, and the pair are photographed again in June, in the Argentine capital, where the national team are playing two qualifiers for the 2010 South Africa World Cup. This time, it's a family photo – Antonella is arm in arm with Leo's mother Celia. Are there wedding bells on the horizon? 'I'm not getting married just yet,' insists Lionel.

Every love story has its ups and downs. In January 2011, during an interview with Rosario Radio 2, Leo's maternal grandfather, Antonio Cuccittini, claims: 'He doesn't have a girlfriend right now, he had one but I think they had a disagreement. It's better, he's very young, I always tell him to just have fun.' But it seems Lionel doesn't intend to follow his grandfather's advice, and hops on a plane from Barcelona to Buenos Aires to Rosario in the middle of the season to see the love of his life. The two return to the Ciudad Condal to start a new life together. And in November 2012, they announce the birth of their first child, Thiago. Three years later there's another announcement, as Mateo is born.

Antonella seems like a down-to-earth girl, who doesn't seek the limelight or pay any attention to the gossip columns. When she has something to say she does it through Instagram, and she knows how to live her life more or less unnoticed, ensuring nothing is said about her that she doesn't want anyone to know. She seems reserved, a trait that runs in her family. Anyone who calls her parents' house in Rosario for an interview is told: 'We are not famous.'

Of course, like Leo she has also undergone quite a transformation that has not escaped the notice of either the press or the fans. Her appearance at the Ballon d'Or gala in January 2016, in a spectacular dress complemented by her permanent smile, was hailed as one of the best. Like her husband, she is evidently more comfortable now at these big events, more sure of herself. Her understated beauty is the perfect reflection of her love story with one of the best footballers in history.

* * *

It's a different world to that of Cristiano Ronaldo's last known and longest relationship, with top model Irina Shayk, who was more famous than he was when they started dating. Born Irina Shaykhlislamova on 6 January 1986 in Yemanzhelinsk, in the Republic of Bashkortostan, Russia, she is a year older than CR7. She is from a modest family: her father, a miner, died when she was just fourteen, and her kindergarten music teacher mother had to take on two jobs to make ends meet. Her life changed when, at the age of eighteen, she accompanied her sister Tatiana to beauty school, and was spotted by someone from a modelling agency who noticed her unusual looks. They encouraged her to enter Miss Chelyabinsk 2004, which she won.

A scout named Guia Jikizde tells her that she could find work as a model in Europe. A year later, Irina is in Paris, signed to the agency Traffic. From there she begins to climb the ranks in the modelling world, becoming the face of Italian lingerie brand Intimissimi in 2007. The same year she appears in a swimsuit edition of *Sports Illustrated*, and on 15 February 2011 she is the first Russian model to make it onto the cover. Meanwhile she has graced the covers of plenty of other fashion magazines, from *GQ, Elle* and *Marie Claire* to *Esquire, Harper's Bazaar* and *Women*. She has also fronted campaigns for La Perla, Guess, Armani, Modellato, Lacoste and Replay, to name just a few.

In the five years that they are together, Irina seems to have managed what none before her could: to get CR7 to settle down and defy the supposed playboy image so fondly attributed to him by the press. The Spanish tabloids and gossip columns have wasted no time linking the footballer with dozens of alleged girlfriends and lovers from the second he arrived from England – from Brazilian model Jordana Jardel to Mallorcan nurse Nereida Gallardo, from Miss Italy Letizia Filippi to Paris Hilton, from British actress Gemma Atkinson to university student Olivia Saunders. But all the speculation ends in spring 2010, when Cristiano meets Irina through mutual friends. By early 2011 he has welcomed her into La Finca, his Madrid mansion.

At the time, Irina says Cristiano is the perfectly supportive partner, always at her side and able to make her happy. He understands the importance of her work. But everything changes at the beginning of 2015. Their separation is all over the front pages, and not just in the tabloids. The sports papers are also bogged down in the details of what happened between one of the most idolised – and bankable – couples in the world.

Portuguese daily *Correio da Manha* claims that it was CR7 who ended things because they hardly ever saw each other and he supposedly 'wants a woman who is always by his side'. There is also talk of an allegedly uneasy relationship between Shayk and the player's mother and sisters. It is even claimed that the break-up has been caused by Shayk's reluctance to attend her mother-in-law's 60th birthday. 'Dolores Aveiro is convinced that Irina was not the right partner for her son,' alleges *Correio*. 'She would prefer someone who is willing in the future to assume the role of mother to little Cristiano, but that wasn't a priority for Irina,' claims the newspaper. And of course, they all want to dig up dirt on Cristiano's supposed infidelities. He opts to remain completely silent on the matter, only releasing an official statement on 20 January via Associated Press to confirm the split: 'After dating for five years, my relationship with Irina Shayk has come to an end. We believed it would be best for both of us to take this step now. I wish Irina the greatest happiness.' He will say nothing further about the matter.

At first, his ex adopts the same approach, communicating only via her agent: 'All negative rumours regarding Irina and Ronaldo's family are completely false and have nothing whatsoever to do with their break-up.' But on 11 February Irina herself hints that the separation may not have been as amicable as previously thought. 'I'm looking for a man who is honest and faithful,' she tells *E! News*. It is unclear if she is referring to CR7. A few weeks later she is even more explicit in an exclusive interview with *¡Hola!* magazine in which she says she felt 'ugly and insecure' while with Cristiano. Once again she emphasises the importance of faithfulness and concludes that she thought she had 'found the idea man … but no.'

The Sun claims to have the inside track on the meaning behind Irina's comments. It alleges that the Portuguese cheated on Irina with at least twelve different women. It claims she supposedly discovered various messages that he had sent to girls in different countries, that he denied it, and that she decided to break things off.

From that moment on, the press are intent on revealing one supposed romance after another. Cristiano is back living the single life, going out and having fun, judging by the photos he posts on his various social networks. Now it's what he gets up to in his free time that is occupying the front pages. In autumn 2015, the press start pouncing on his frequent trips to Marrakesh, particularly after he posts pictures online in the company of Moroccan professional kickboxer and martial artist Badr Hari. There is nothing particular of note, but as always there are some who want to analyse every detail: the two men pictured arm in arm … in one shot Hari is carrying the player with the jokey caption 'Just Married' … in another they are surrounded by an all-male group of friends. In the pool, sunbathing, having dinner, and on a second hand private jet that the footballer bought for 19 million euros for these short getaways. And the ones who aren't interested in sentimental allusions instead focus on pointing out that Hari could be a bad influence on someone who has such a squeaky clean lifestyle.

Dolores Aveiro is the first to defend her son. 'He has to live his life,' she says.

* * *

The same could be said about Neymar Júnior since his split with Bruna Reis Maia. Born on 4 March 1995 in Duque de Caixas, Rio de Janeiro state, Neymar's former girlfriend is better known as Bruna Marquezine, the stage name she inherited from her grandfather. Her TV advertising career began at the tender age of four, and she went on to appear on *Gente Inocente* – '*Innocent People*', a popular programme presented at the time by Márcio Garcia, in which children interviewed celebrities as well as showcasing their own singing, acting and dancing talents.

At eight she dazzles the nation as Salete in the telenovela *Mulheres Apaixonadas* – 'Passionate Women'. 'I didn't know how to read. My mother Neide used to read me the scripts and I would learn them,' Bruna recently revealed. Two years later she is cast as María Flor in another soap, *America*, which is followed by roles on *Cobras y Lagartos, Desejo Proibido, Negócio da China, Araguaia, Aquele Beijo, Rio del Destino and Salve Jorge.* The child prodigy has grown up and become a star – and not just on the Globo TV network, where she most recently appeared in yet another prime time soap, *En Familia* – but across the whole of Brazil. And she has managed to do it all without losing her innocent nature along the way. Not for nothing does she have 1.4 million Instagram followers.

Rumours linking her to Brazil's newest football icon surface in September 2012. The first snaps of the pair appear in the Brazilian tabloids in October, when they are spotted at a Claudia Leitte concert in Rio. But neither will confirm the supposed romance. It is not until February 2013 that Neymar finally confesses all to the press at the Rio Carnival. 'It's 100 per cent official, it's true,' he says, explaining that they have only been together for a month, whereas they were just friends when the photos were published in October. A week later Bruna goes to Santos to watch the Peixe play. A week after that Neymar heads to Rio to watch Bruna dance in the famous Grande Rio carnival parade. It is understood that they met after Neymar obtained the actress's phone number through a mutual friend, and from there, romance blossomed.

From the minute the relationship becomes public knowledge, the two cannot escape the photographers, but they are careful to protect their privacy, sticking mainly to declarations of love via Instagram. And when asked whether their relationship can work across thousands of miles, Bruna replies: 'Distance is not an obstacle. We see each other often, although we don't publicise the fact. I miss him, he is very romantic.'

On 29 September 2013, she appears on *Domingão do Faustão* – 'Big Fausto's Big Sunday', a well-known Brazilian TV talk show hosted every Sunday by Fausto Silva since 1989. They connect live to Barcelona, and a grinning Neymar appears on screen in his backwards baseball cap. He is full of praise for Bruna, who has just lost out in the final of the Brazilian version of *Dancing with the Stars*. 'I was with her all the way,' he says. 'As far as I'm concerned, she's a ten, and I would crown her the champion.' The Barça number 11 also speaks of feeling homesick, of his sadness at not being able to share these moments with her: 'It's tough, although it was always tough because Santos and Rio are also far apart, but now the distance is that much greater. I miss you! But our love can survive this and I hope that you'll come here soon. I just wanted to tell you that I love you.' Then he jokes to Fausto to 'let her go!' so that she can come over. After he is gone, the cameras focus on Bruna, who cannot contain her tears.

But the love story ends just a few months later. On 11 February 2014, Bruna confirms via her publicist that her relationship with Neymar is over. Brazilian newspaper *O Globo* alleges that distance was one of the key factors in their break-up.

Sometime later, the player acknowledges that 'no break-up is easy, but it was the best thing for both of us. Bruna and I are still friends, and we still speak from time to time.'

Chapter 10

Kids

All three became fathers very young, Neymar at nineteen, Messi and Ronaldo at 25, but under very different circumstances.

For Neymar it was a surprise, for Leo it was with his long-term partner, while Ronaldo's story has been the subject of much speculation.

On 3 July 2010 Cristiano announces on Facebook and Twitter that he has become a father. 'It is with great joy and emotion that I inform I have recently become father to a baby boy. As agreed with the baby's mother, who prefers to have her identity kept confidential, my son will be under my exclusive guardianship. No further information will be provided on this subject and I request everyone to fully respect my right to privacy (and that of the child) at least on issues as personal as these are.'

The Real number 7 shocks the world with his statement, which comes just a few days after Portugal's elimination from the South Africa World Cup. It is a complete surprise because no one even knew that he was in any kind of long-term relationship, let alone expecting. On holiday with Irina in New York, Cristiano has nothing further to say on the matter. It is his sister Katia who speaks out from Marina de Vilamoura in the Algarve, saying: 'Cristiano is very, very happy. What father wouldn't be?' Regarding the baby, she says, 'He has dark eyes and brown hair like Cristiano and he is very well settled – he just eats and sleeps.'

Portuguese television channel RTP announces that he is called Cristiano Junior, and that at birth he measured 53 centimetres and weighed 4.3 kilograms. He was born on 17 June, two days after his father played with the national team against the Ivory Coast in South Africa. This is undoubtedly all useful information, but what really interests the British tabloids, the celebrity magazines and the Portuguese media is the mystery surrounding the mother. Who is she? Why has she relinquished custody of the child? The conspiracy theories are flowing thick and fast.

Portuguese daily newspaper *Diário de Notícias* claims that the baby was conceived artificially the previous year in San Diego, with the help of an American surrogate – around the time that the footballer was on holiday in California and was seen out celebrating his Real Madrid signing with Paris Hilton at a private party in Los Angeles. The paper claims that Cristiano's mother Dolores and his sisters Katia and Elma came to the States to deal with the legal proceedings that would allow them to take the baby back to Portugal.

The tabloid *Correio da Manhã* claims Cristiano Ronaldo has paid to have a baby, while *The Sun* alleges the player has shelled out no fewer than 16 million euros to buy the silence of the mother and ensure that she would give up her right to see the child. That's just one theory. Other Portuguese media speculate that Cristiano Junior is the product of a one-night stand and that the young mother wants nothing to do with the baby.

The soap opera doesn't end there. Six months later, the *Daily Mirror* announces that the identity of the woman who gave birth to the Real number 7's son has been discovered. According to the tabloid, she is a twenty-year-old student from London. It's a theory which Cristiano's ex-girlfriend Nereida Gallardo supports in a Spanish TV interview. The model from Mallorca alleges that the girl contacted her on Facebook months before the birth was announced, claiming that she was expecting Cristiano's child. Months later, the press allege that the girl regrets having given up custody of the child and says she is ready to fight to get him back. Sources who claim to be close to the girl tell the media: 'She feels as if she has sold her soul. She is living like a millionaire, but she will never be able to tell her friends and family what happened and that makes her feel extremely lonely.'

But the plot is about to thicken once again. In an interview with *The Sun*, Katia adds to the mystery. 'There is no woman calling. There is no mother here, there are no phone calls, nothing,' she says. 'The mother has died. The baby has no mother. The child is ours. I am not going to comment on how he came into the world, but I can guarantee you that he is my brother's son, my nephew, our flesh and blood. My mother is now his mother – she is the one who looks after him 24 hours a day.'

The first photos of little Cristiano, published exclusively in the Portuguese magazine *TV Mais*, show him in his grandmother's arms. The baby's face is deliberately pixelated, but it is possible to make out a child with dark skin tones and similar characteristics to his father. Grandma Dolores is taking care of him at Cristiano's home in Madrid. On 8 December, she takes him to the Bernabéu to watch his father play for the first time. Ronaldo has already dedicated various goals to his son. But this is a special occasion. In the 50th minute, after scoring Real's second goal of the night against Auxerre in the Champions League group match, he mimes sucking on a dummy and waves in the direction of the private box. The cameras catch a glimpse of the boy and at that moment Cristiano Junior steals the limelight from his father. All eyes in the stadium are on the baby.

Shortly afterwards, the number 7 breaks his silence

over his recent fatherhood in an interview with Real Madrid TV. He admits that becoming a father has changed him: 'It's a different type of responsibility. I am still learning. It's a feeling I can't easily put into words. Waking up in the morning and seeing some-one who is your own flesh and blood is amazing. This is a very special time in my life. You could say that I am feeling very content. I am always happier when things are going well – with my family, the club, my friends …' Sometime later he breaks the silence again to reveal an unexpected detail about the mother: she is Portuguese, not American as had been rumoured, although that's all he will say on the matter.

Instead, he reassures everyone he has no problem taking on the role of a hands-on father: 'Of course I change my son's nappies. It's not my favourite thing in the world, but I do it.' He talks about the future, the possibility of more children, marriage, and what he would like his son to do when he grows up: 'I would love for him to play football and be my successor, but let's wait and see. My son will be whoever he wants to be.' And he says that, although Cristiano Junior usu-ally goes to sleep without any problem, on one occa-sion when his father was playing a match he cried all day, and they couldn't get him to calm down and go to sleep until he had seen his daddy score a goal.

The world has seen Cristiano Junior grow up through the photographs and videos that CR7 posts of him online. Father and son share the same interests, poses, and often, the same dress sense. 'The experience of having Cristiano has been incredible. Never in my life could I have imagined it would change me so much. It was a dream for me to have a child so young, at 25. It has changed my way of thinking, he is always with me, supporting me.' He insists his son is a very independent child, and although he doubts he would ever support any team other than Real Madrid – 'Barça fan? Impossible! He's got his daddy's genes!' – if it happened, he would accept it.

The little boy splits his time between his father and his grandmother. On 13 January 2014 he accompanies them to Zurich where the Real star wins the Ballon d'Or after waiting for several years. As he goes up on stage to collect his trophy, his son runs up behind him with an enormous smile on his face. It's all too much for the player, who cannot stop crying, while Junior won't let go of his father. The following year, just before he collects the trophy for the second year running, the little boy sparks the anecdote of the night. Moments before the ceremony, father and son are waiting in the same room as Leo Messi. 'He watches your matches and he talks about you,' the Real star tells his Barça rival, in an encounter that leaves the four-and-a-half-year-old speechless.

* * *

'I think Thiago is right-footed. The first time he kicked with his left, I was overjoyed. In all honesty it's hard to tell. But when it comes to choosing between a film and football, he prefers the ball,' says a proud Leo Messi, whose son turned one on 2 November 2013. The announcement of the impending arrival came, of course, on the pitch, when after scoring Argentina's third goal against Ecuador in a World Cup qualifier in June 2012 Messi put the ball under his shirt, pretending to be pregnant. A lovely tribute to Antonella, mother of his future child.

A few days before the birth, the Barça number 10 wins his second Golden Boot for being the highest goal-scorer in a European league in the 2011–12 season. The 1960 Ballon d'Or winner Luis Suárez Miramontes presents the trophy on 29 October at the old Estrella Damm factory in Barcelona. Oscar Campillo, director of sports magazine *Marca*, goes up on stage and reveals the Golden Boot's 'little brother' – a mini golden bootie and golden dummy, and presents them to Messi as a gift for the forthcoming baby.

At 5.14pm on Friday 2 November 2012, Thiago is born at the ISP Dexeus hospital, close to the Nou Camp. Leo's little sister María Sol is tasked with sharing the news with the world. Half an hour later, she tweets: 'Welcome little Thiaaaago!!' Messi is a dad. He had accompanied Antonella to the maternity ward at 9am, where they were given a private suite on the seventh floor so that the whole family could have the maximum possible privacy. Jorge, Celia, Matías, Rodrigo and María Sol had arrived at around 3pm – along with the media. Leo is by Antonella's side and assists with the delivery. Everything goes well and both mother and baby are healthy. At 6.20pm, Leo posts on Facebook: 'Today I am the happiest man in the world, my son was born and thanks to God for this gift! Thanks to my family for the support! A hug to everyone.'

Leo has missed training to be with his partner of four years, but the following day he starts in a Liga match against Celta Vigo. He is particularly moti-vated, as he wants to dedicate a goal to Thiago. At the Golden Boot presentation he had said: 'I'll do something special when I score the first goal, but then it'll be back to normal.' But despite all his best efforts, he doesn't score against Celta. The dummy in his left sock that he wanted to use in a celebration stays put. 'We tried to help him as always, particularly today, but it just wasn't happening,' says Pedro. Iniesta adds: 'It would have been lovely for him and for all of us, but he'll have another chance on Wednesday.'

On Wednesday 7 November against Celtic in Glasgow Leo scores in injury time and sticks his thumb in his mouth in tribute to his son. When asked why he chose such a low-key celebration, he explains: 'The goal didn't really do much [Barcelona lose 2-1]. There will be other chances to dedicate goals to him.' Plenty of other chances. On Sunday 11 November against Mallorca in La Liga, he is able to celebrate two goals, a victory and the birth in the way he wants. And against Levante, he wears a wristband that reads 'I love you Thiago', which he kisses after scoring each of his two goals.

'I have changed in every way. It was a question of mindset. That came first, and everything else followed. It has changed the way I view a match. Before, if we lost or I played badly I wouldn't talk to anyone for three or four days while I got over the frustration. Now if we lose, I go home and see my son and I can let go. I might still be angry on the inside, but seeing him changes everything. Being a father has helped me grow up. It has helped me to stop being so obsessed over football and to realise that there are other things in life too.' Leo Messi speaks with emotion about his firstborn, whose arrival brought about a shift in many ways. He has been more open to showing his feelings, and has become even more close-knit, especially since the arrival of Mateo, the fourth member of the family.

On 11 September 2015 Antonella gives birth to the couple's second son. The Flea still doesn't have a Twitter account, so his brother Matías gets the honour of posting the news. 'Hi everyone, MATEO HAS ARRIVED! He's gorgeous. More details later, right

now we're just enjoying him!!! Thank you everyone!!!'
Antonella posts the first photo of the little one on
Instagram, a black and white snapshot of baby and
mother's hands, with the sweet caption: 'Welcome my
little boy! We are so happy to have you here with us!
We love you! Daddy, Thiagui and Mummy ❤❤❤ #fam-
ilyof4.' Leo has missed training to be by Antonella's
side during the birth, but he's back at work the following day to face Atlético Madrid at the Calderón. He
starts on the bench for the first time in nearly a year,
but at least this time it's not because of a misunder-
standing with the coach. He comes on during the last
half hour when the teams are tied 1-1, and suddenly
the match comes alive. Atlético are intimidated by his
presence, and sixteen minutes later he scores the victory goal, sucking his thumb in celebration as a tribute
to the new arrival.

* * *

Neymar's little blonde boy is born on 24 August 2011
in São Luiz hospital in São Paulo. Neymar announces
it with a tweet, accompanied by a picture of himself
enveloped in an orange hospital gown and white
scrub cap, holding the baby. Another picture follows,
this time with his friend Paulo Henrique, the baby's
godfather. He also posts a message on his website in
Portuguese, English and Spanish confirming that both
mother and newborn are doing well. 'He is 2.81 kilos

of *pure joy*. We are very grateful to God for this *blessing in our lives.*'

But despite assuring the world that David Lucca is the most important and best thing to have happened to him, becoming a father at nineteen can't have been easy. When he finds out that sixteen-year-old Carolina Dantas is expecting, Neymar is faced with a role of significant responsibility – with someone whom he had only met through mutual friends and dated briefly. She decides that her baby will want to know who his father is, so she breaks the news to Juninho, who behaves 'like the perfect gentleman', she will later acknowledge on Faustão's Sunday chat show. But they still have to broach the issue with their families. Neymar's mother Nadine is emotional upon hearing the news. It's tougher with his father, who has always been the one to warn him to tread carefully in life. But despite the circumstances, the conversation ends with a hug and the advice that his son should accept his responsibilities and view being a father as a wonderful thing. Whether or not Neymar decides to be with Carolina, Neymar Pai looks forward to having a grandchild, and goes with his son to visit the Dantas family.

It is decided that the mother will have custody of the child, and will receive monthly support to help with his upbringing. Neymar goes public with the news – although without revealing the mother's identity at this stage. He supports Carolina throughout the pregnancy, and is there in the delivery room to welcome David Lucca into the world at 11am on 24 August. 'Juninho is a wonderful father – considerate, attentive, and a good friend who supports me through everything,' says medical student Carolina. 'When he was at Santos, he came to see David whenever he could, he showers him with gifts and attention, and he has often stayed over at our house so that he could spend more time with him.'

First Neymar presents his son to the world at the Peniel Baptist Church, and then, on 7 September, at just two weeks old, he takes him to the CT Rei Pelé – the Santos training ground – to introduce him to his teammates. On 4 March 2012 he makes quite an entrance with little David at the Vila Belmiro for the Santos–Corinthians derby. The kid gets a kiss from godfather Henrique, and brings the team a bit of luck in their 1-0 victory.

'Davi really resembles his father. And if he has so much as a cold, Neymar is always really worried. Whatever the problem, he always helps out,' says Carolina. But the first few months at Barcelona are not easy for the star. The distance between him and his son is too great. 'I would love to meet someone, get married, have children, it's something I've always talked about with my friends, I've got that girly dream of getting married in a church, having the big party with all the friends, then having a family, having my children by my side every day. I have a son who lives far away and I know how difficult that is. I still have that yearning to be a family man,' he explains in an interview with Seleçao SporTV.

Ney lives with the heartache, although he always finds a way to stay in touch. 'Every six to eight weeks he comes to Barcelona. It's difficult being away from the kid, it makes me very wistful. I speak to him almost every day, on his mum's mobile or I send him voice-mails, to try to alleviate the sadness I feel from being so far away.'

In the summer of 2015, the striker and his ex-partner demonstrate just how strong a relationship they have maintained, making a crucial decision: she and the little one will come and live in Barcelona, in a house owned by Neymar, so that father and son can be nearer each other. 'I thank God every day for making me a father. I am still learning, and he still surprises me every day,' the *Blaugrana* number 11 posts on Instagram. 'Son, I hope God always guides you in life. Daddy loves you.'

Chapter 11

Duels

Throughout the history of sport, there have always been duels. A one-on-one battle is all part of the experience that stirs up and divides fans across the world. Boxers Ali and Frazier, racing drivers Prost and Senna, golfers Mickelson and Woods, tennis stars McEnroe and Borg or Federer and Nadal, basketball players Magic Johnson and Larry Bird, or Stephen Curry and LeBron James, motorcycle racers Valentino Rossi and Marc Márquez, athletes Carl Lewis and Ben Johnson, pole vaulters Sergey Bubka and Thierry Vigneron ... the list is endless.

But in football, it is rare to find a player considered to be a 'great' who can also be overshadowed by a contemporary. Pelé, Cruyff, Maradona and Di Stéfano never overlapped in terms of their time at the top – unlike Lionel Messi and Cristiano Ronaldo, whose rivalry was inevitable even before they were playing in the same league. But the challenge to be crowned world number one has intensified ever since CR7 moved to Real in 2009.

But what do the men in question think? 'It's not a personal duel with Leo,' insists Cristiano. 'Each of us works hard and gives it our all.' 'He's right,' says Messi, 'We just try to do the best we can and help our teams win.' They have said it time and again – in various different ways. Cristiano, for example, has previously declared: 'I don't compete against Messi, I compete against myself and against all the teams in La Liga.' It's true to an extent that Cristiano likes to compete with himself, but there is no doubt Leo is something of an Achilles' heel for him. It's not a coincidence that from Spain, to Cyprus, to Bosnia, rival fans chant 'Messi, Messi, Messi!' at him. They know it will touch a nerve.

Leo has been compared with Cristiano for years. He is seen as his direct rival in the race to become the best in the world. But Cristiano actually makes it to the top first, winning France Football's Ballon d'Or in 2008 while still at Man United – before Messi. He also takes home the Golden Boot for top scorer in a European league. 'No one could legitimately dispute that Ronaldo has developed into the world's most devastating attacker,' writes the *Guardian* in its 2007–08 season round-up. And he has won his first big duel against Leo. It's true that on 23 April 2008 against Barça at the Nou Camp in the semi-final of the Champions League, Cristiano misses a penalty in the second minute. But thanks to a single goal from Paul

Scholes, the Red Devils are on their way to Moscow, where they win the title.

But the tables are turned the following year, when Messi helps Barça seal the deal in the Champions League final in Rome, marking the beginning of his run of trophies, and knocking CR7 off the number one spot. After that, the Argentine wins four consecutive Ballon d'Or prizes, overtaking legends Johan Cruyff, Marco van Basten and Michel Platini, who have three wins apiece. By 7 January 2013, Cristiano's frustration is evident as Messi takes to the stage in Zurich in a black and white polka dot Dolce & Gabbana jacket and bow tie to receive his fourth trophy from Fabio Cannavaro. The Barça number 10 has beaten Ronaldo yet again, squeezing him into second place.

Given the history, it is therefore easy to understand CR7's tearful reaction a year later, on 13 January 2014, when he finally reclaims the Holy Grail, the prize that reinstates him as the greatest player in the world. He has beaten Messi, despite not having won any titles in 2013 – it is all down to his individual performance and his 69 goals.

A year later, he does it again. This time there are no tears for Cristiano, just a guttural roar of YEEEEEESSSSSSSSSSS!! which surprises the audience. It's his third Ballon d'Or and he celebrates as if he's scored a trophy-winning goal. The roar is for his teammates' benefit – it's his battle cry. He's unleashed it before, during training and some matches, although tonight it's as though they're hearing it for the first time, and it certainly provokes a reaction on social media. Nothing can ruin the Portuguese's night – not even the knowledge that he wasn't then FIFA president Sepp Blatter's favourite for the award, nor then UEFA president Michel Platini's. Nor was he the top choice of presenter Thierry Henry, who reads out his name in a rather impassive tone. Blatter and Platini preferred Bayern Munich goalie Manuel Neuer, who helped Germany win the 2014 World Cup, while Henry favoured his old Barça team-mate Messi. But even without their backing, Ronaldo has received 37.66% of the votes, more than his two rivals combined. Messi has just 15.76% and Neuer 15.72%. CR7 doesn't hide the fact that he aspires to win more. 'I don't want to tread water, I want to do as well as Messi. He hasn't thwarted my dreams, rather he has inspired me.' Leo is his reference point, the mirror he holds up against his own achievements.

But twelve months later the tables have turned, as the Rosarino reclaims his throne in Zurich on 11 January 2016. Lionel arrives as the strong favourite to win his fifth trophy after a two-year drought. 'I'm not surprised to be here, but Leo has the edge because his team won all the titles,' concedes the Portuguese at the pre-ceremony press conference. Ever since they saw each other at the last gala a year ago, there has been a better understanding between the two. All the old tension is gone. And when CR7 is asked which of the Argentine's skills he would take if he had the choice, he quips: 'His left foot isn't bad. I think it's a bit better than mine.' They both grin. And just to dispel any lingering doubts, the Barça star says: 'We have always had a good relationship. We're colleagues, we just don't have daily contact because we play at different clubs. But there has always been respect and admiration on both sides.'

They are sitting next to each other during the ceremony, and there is no surprise when Leo is revealed as the winner, but there are no negative reactions either. The Argentine has 41 per cent of the votes to Cristiano's 27 and Neymar's 7. Yes, for the first time, Ney Júnior is seated between the world's top players, making small talk, just two and a half years after arriving at Barcelona. He knew it would be mission impossible to win the Ballon d'Or on this occasion, but everyone at the Zurich gala knows that the Brazilian will have his time to shine in the future. 'I never played to be the best in the world or to win the Ballon d'Or,' says the Barça number 11. 'I always played to be the best I could be, to push myself further. Being the best in the world is a result of that hard work. If I am here talking about this today, it's because my work is paying off.'

There had been calls for Barcelona's MSN 'trident'

of Messi, Suárez and Neymar to all be nominated. But at the gala in Switzerland Neymar praises not only Leo's genius, but also that of his rival CR7. 'I don't know who is better, Messi or Cristiano, but I admire them both greatly. I have watched them both play since I was young, and it is incredible to be able to be here with them. They each have their own story and their own achievements. They are the greatest players I have ever seen and they have both made history. I see Leo every day and I admire him as a player and as a person. He is very calm and he's a good friend. Cristiano I have followed more on TV. But they have both enjoyed great success for around eight or nine years now, and one day I hope to be like them – in a position to break my own records.' It's his first real taste of the action, and the Brazilian doesn't try to hide his ambition, saying, 'I hope to be back.'

Ballon d'Or trophies aside, CR7 versus Messi – and now with Neymar added into the mix as a third challenger – has earned its place in footballing history as a classic derby of its own, a rivalry that has provided some unforgettable moments over the last six years. Both are leaders of their respective teams, and they are undoubtedly the stars of La Liga and the European footballing landscape as a whole.

In 2009–10, Cristiano's first season with Real, Leo is the Liga top scorer with 34, while Ronaldo scores 26. With 47 goals across all tournaments, Messi also wins the Golden Boot. The Argentine is decisive in both *Clásico* derbies against Real, and Barça go on to win La Liga.

In 2010–11, however, Cristiano tops the Liga goal-scoring tables with 40 in 34 matches, and also clinches the Golden Boot. He has scored more goals than some entire Liga teams – Sporting de Gijón have managed 35, Deportivo de La Coruña 31, and Hércules and Almería 36 each. And compared with other championships outside Spain, his stats are on another level. He has scored almost as many goals as the two top scorers of the Premier League put together, Man United's Berbatov and Manchester City's Tévez, who each scored 21. Between La Liga, the Copa del Rey and the Champions League, he has scored 53 – the same as Messi. They have beaten the highest goal-scorer in a season record set by Puskás, who netted 49 in the 1959–60 season.

For the third year running Messi is the Champions League top scorer with twelve goals, and he has helped Barça win La Liga, the Champions League and the Club World Cup. Cristiano has to console himself with the Copa del Rey, his first title with Real. The two have come face-to-face six times in the season: five derbies – two in La Liga, two in the Champions League semis, and the Copa del Rey final – and one friendly between Portugal and Argentina. Three wins for Leo, one for Cristiano and two draws.

On to 2011–12, and 'the battle for La Liga isn't about two teams, it's about two players,' claims the *Sport* editorial the night before the Barcelona–Real Madrid match on 21 April 2012. Over 32 matches, Messi and Ronaldo have each notched up 41 goals, topping the Portuguese's record from the previous season. Leo has managed five hat-tricks, one four-goal game and six doubles. Cristiano has scored six hat-tricks and five doubles. 'You have never seen anything like it,' continues *Sport*. 'Never has La Liga had two such phenomenal players.' Two phenomenal players who are about to compete for the title. It should be noted that Cristiano was on the losing side in the last Liga *Clásico*, on 10 December 2011, when Barça trounced the Whites at the Bernabéu 3-1. But he will make up for it this time, scoring the winning goal in Real's 2-1 victory, crowning them Liga champions.

After three seasons at Real, the Madrid press rejoices at Cristiano's 'dethroning' of Messi. But the Argentine is still the Liga top scorer with 50 goals – a new record. At the end of the season he will have racked up an incredible 73, and he will make it 91 by the end of the calendar year. Cristiano has 'only' scored 60 in the season, including 46 in La Liga. But he becomes the first footballer in history to have scored more than 40 Liga goals in two consecutive seasons. And he's the only player to have scored against every single other team in La Liga.

The 2012–13 season kicks off with another *Clásico* – this time in the Spanish Supercup. The first leg is at the Nou Camp on 23 August 2012, and finishes 3-2 to the home team. Cristiano opens the scoring with a header, while Messi nets Barça's second from the penalty spot. The decider is six days later at the Bernabéu. Ronaldo scores for Real, taking it to 2-0. Messi has been quiet during the first half, but after half time he scores from a free kick, throwing the game wide open once again. Real are struggling, but they manage to hold on and take home their first title of the season, leaving Messi and Barça on the sidelines. They will come face-to-face once again on 7 October, in another Liga *Clásico*, this time at the Nou Camp. By now Cristiano has scored twelve goals, eight of them in the last four matches, including two hat-tricks – one against Ajax in the Champions League and the other in La Liga against Deportivo de La Coruña. Messi has scored ten, but none in the last three matches. This time they are both on form, scoring two goals each and putting on a stunning, intense performance that delights not only the fans at the ground, but also the 400 million live TV viewers. 'Out of this world', reads the *Marca* headline the following day, adding: 'Messi and CR7 show with their doubles why they are from another planet.'

By the end of the season, Real have won another *Clásico* – their first derby triumph at the Bernabéu since the 2007–08 season. Cristiano has scored 55 goals in 55 matches – 34 in La Liga in 34 matches, seven in the Copa del Rey, two in the Supercup and twelve in the Champions League in as many games. Meanwhile Messi has scored 60 in 50 matches. His 46 La Liga goals win him another highest scorer accolade, and, of course, there is another Ballon d'Or in his trophy cabinet.

The 2013–14 season introduces a new factor into the Real-Barça/Cristiano-Messi duel. Now Neymar is part of the equation. Wearing the *Blaugrana* colours, and despite still being some way behind his two 'maestros', he is starting to make himself noticed on the pitch. In fact, the Brazilian is the star of the show in his first *Clásico* against Real at the Nou Camp on 26 October 2013. He has his opponents despairing during the full 90 minutes, he is unstoppable in his one-on-ones, and gets his team off the mark in the eighteenth minute. Not only that, he also sets up a goal for Alexis in the final fifteen minutes of the match. It ends 2-1 to Barça, and everyone is talking about him. The two teams will come face to face again in La Liga on 23 March 2014 at the Santiago Bernabéu. Ney doesn't score this time, but both Messi and Cristiano do. The Argentine nets three out of his team's four goals, while the Portuguese has to console himself with a single goal from the penalty spot. By the time the referee blows the whistle it's an impressive 3-4, and Barça have managed to overtake the Whites.

And they are back at it barely a month later, this time in the final of the Copa del Rey in Mestalla, which Real win with a resounding performance, 3-0. Without a doubt, the image of the night is … Cristiano consoling Messi. The Portuguese has not been playing due to injury niggles, but that doesn't stop him going up to the Argentine to try to cheer him up.

The next time the three of them meet on the pitch is on 25 October 2014 at the Bernabéu. For the first time, the match unites Barcelona's new strikeforce of Neymar, Messi and Uruguayan Luis Suárez, who debuts with his new team after an eight-match ban for biting Italy defender Giorgio Chiellini during the World Cup. But the triple aces are rendered powerless against the Real effect, and the Whites take the first duel of the season, 3-1. The consolation Barça goal goes to Ney – it's the first goal of the match and it seems to hint at an easy victory. But Ronaldo mounts the comeback, followed by Pepe and Benzema. The roles are reversed on 22 March 2015, the second *Clásico* of the season, as the rival teams head out onto the Nou Camp pitch at 9pm. This time it's the Whites who start off well, but in the eighteenth minute the *Blaugrana* take advantage of a dead ball to get ahead. Messi passes to Mathieu, who heads it in to make it 1-0. Cristiano gets the equaliser, but ten minutes after the half time break Suárez makes it a definitive 2-1. Leo doesn't score, but he does set a record for the most assists in the history of the *Clásico*. Ney has also made a very good impression.

Just as he does eight months later in the 2015–16 season. It's Saturday 21 November, and Barça are away to Real. Leo has been given the all clear by the medics after six weeks out due to injury, although he is still starting on the bench. He comes on in the second half and the Messi-Suárez-Neymar 'MSN' trident is finally reunited. And they don't disappoint, crushing their eternal rivals 0-4. Ney scores the second in the 39th minute with an outstanding play.

With the memory of that triumph still fresh, Barça go out onto the Nou Camp pitch on 2 April, just a few days after the death of legendary *Blaugrana* player and coach Johan Cruyff. It's a blow for the whole team, who hope to be able to pay tribute to him with a resounding victory over Real in the second *Clásico* of the season. The game starts with a video honouring the late footballer, and a mosaic created by the fans in the stands, depicting his number 14 shirt and the words 'Graciès Johan'. Unfortunately, the result gives them no cause for celebration. The locals go one up in the 55th minute, but Real manage to get back on track thanks to a Karim Benzema equaliser in the 62nd minute. And a stunning shot from Cristiano takes it to 1-2: he gets the ball from Gareth Bale, controls it perfectly on his chest on the edge of the box, and shoots, sliding the ball under the legs of goalie Claudio Bravo.

Real have succeeded in breaking a run of 39 games without loss for the *Blaugrana*, who until that moment seemed unstoppable. The Whites are fired up, their honour is restored, and suddenly they are back in the race for a La Liga that previously looked to be all sewn up. In the end, Messi and Ney will win it on the last day of the season.

Chapter 12

Numbers

'I asked whether the number 28 shirt, which I wore at Sporting Lisbon, was available. Alex Ferguson said to me, "No no, yours is the number 7." "Ok boss!" I replied. I wasn't going to say to him, "No no, mine is the number 28."' Cristiano Ronaldo describes how he came to wear the famous number 7 at Manchester United, worn by all the great Red Devils players before him: George Best, Steve Coppel, Bryan Robson, Eric Cantona and David Beckham.

But how did such a young new signing get to don such an important shirt number in the club's history?

Here's how Sir Alex explains the motives behind his decision to the press: 'We have given Ronaldo this shirt because he is young and he is going to do great things. A number of great players in the club's history have worn this shirt. Ronaldo has great confidence in his abilities and he is going to be here for a while. The number 7 shirt is his.'

'The number 7 shirt is an honour and a responsibility,' replies Cristiano. 'I hope it brings me a lot of luck.' And to the Portuguese press he explains: 'Everyone in Manchester has been telling me about Best and Cantona ... I'm proud to follow in their footsteps. But there's something that the Brits don't know – number 7 is also special to me because it's the number that Luís Figo wore at Sporting. I have wanted to be like him since I was a little kid and wear the number 7.'

Seven goes on to become something of a magic number for Cristiano.. But when he arrives at Real Madrid in 2009, the lucky number is not available – it belongs to Raúl González Blanco, and Cristiano has to content himself with the number 9, once worn by another great Ronaldo before him. When asked about it, he shrugs it off: 'I'm concerned about playing well, not about the number. I'm the one that's playing, not the number on my back.'

But when Raúl leaves Real for FC Schalke 04 in 2010, Ronaldo doesn't hesitate at the opportunity to reclaim his favourite number, which he has also been wearing for Portugal. CR7 is a brand in its own right, recognised across the world. It is even the name of the player's latest underwear collection and is used as a logo on his line of sportswear.

Neymar Júnior also knows a thing or two about the power of the number 7. On Sunday 15 March 2009 Santos face Mogi Mirim, Rivaldo's former team, at the Pacaembu stadium. Coach Vágner Mancini is missing five players, so he puts Neymar in the starting line-up, wearing the number 7.

In the seventeenth minute Neymar gets his first chance. He pushes forward into the box, gets past one defender and tries to shoot across the goal. Goalkeeper Marcelo Cruz blocks it. In the 35th minute Henrique takes a stunning shot but defender Júlio César deflects it. Santos won't take the lead until the second half, when Henrique and Roni make it 2-0. But there is no time to relax, the team keeps up the pressure until, five minutes later, in the 73rd minute, Neymar nets his first goal. The play begins deep in the Santos half. Molina moves up the midfield and crosses to Germano, who sends it out wide on the left to Triguinho, who gets into the box and crosses into the middle, where Neymar beats Cruz with a header. It is 6.37pm and Santos are 3-0 up.

It's a date marked by the number 7, the same number Neymar wore from a young age at school playing futsal. And it's the number worn by his friend and idol Robinho. But it's not his lucky number – he prefers 11 and 10. He likes 11 because of Antônio Lima dos Santos, the Santos player who entertained the world in the 1960s, and coached Neymar in the Peixe youth teams. One day he asked him: 'What number would you like to wear?' The kid thought for a minute and then shyly replied: 'I'd like to wear number 11.' Since then he has achieved his greatest triumphs at Santos in the number 11, has debuted in it for the national team, and has been doing well in it at Barcelona.

As for number 10, he first wore it to play futsal for Gremetal when he was very little. Fifteen years later on 2 June 2013, in a friendly against England at the new Maracaná stadium, Luiz Felipe Scolari gives him the yellow number 10 shirt, the number worn by Pelé for many years. It's a gesture that demonstrates the Brazilian coach's confidence and trust in Neymar as a team leader – and Neymar goes on to lead the team to victory in the FIFA Confederations Cup.

Interestingly, Neymar has used many other numbers during his career: 21 when he was fifteen and he came on to play in the Copa São Paulo Juniores, 23 in a friendly in December 2006, 100 and 200 when he celebrated his 100th and 200th matches with Santos, and even 360 in March 2013 to launch a publicity campaign.

When it comes to Leo Messi, on the other hand, it's difficult to imagine him wearing anything but the number 10. It's his number at Barça and with the Argentine Albiceleste. He first wore it when he dribbled the ball across the Newell's Old Boys pitch as a little boy. But he had a long journey to reclaim it. In his debut with the Barça first team on 16 November 2003, at sixteen years, four months and 23 days, in a friendly against Porto at the Dragão stadium, he wore number 14. At Stamford Bridge on 22 February 2006 in the first leg of the final sixteen of the Champions League against José Mourinho's Chelsea, he wore a bright yellow shirt bearing the number 30. It's an unusual number, but it's a spectacular match that earns him recognition among the world's greatest players.

Finally, on 3 August 2008 he inherits the number 10 shirt at Barça from Ronaldinho, who has departed for AC Milan. He takes up the mantle of a number worn by the likes of Maradona, Romário, Rivaldo, Hugo Sotil and Luis Suárez, accepting without hesitation the responsibility that it implies and, with it, becoming a Barça standard-bearer.

It's just as interesting a journey with the Argentine team. He debuts with the Under 20s wearing number 17, then switches to 18 for the Sudamericano tournament and the Under 20 World Cup, which he later wears for his first – rather unlucky – match with the first team against Hungary on 17 August 2005. For the 2006 World Cup he wears number 19. It is to be Diego Armando Maradona, coach for the 2010 South Africa World Cup, who offers him the prized number 10 – the same number he himself wore when he scored the goal of the century in the 1986 World Cup in Mexico.

Chapter 13

Money

'There are more important things in life than money. It's important, yes, but it's not the main priority,' Cristiano Ronaldo says, upon renewing his contract with Real Madrid on 15 September 2013. That is his response to the possibility of becoming the highest paid footballer on the planet.

Of course, if one were to ask Lionel, he would say the same as the Portuguese. But the fact is that each time one of them signs or renews a contract, it has an ever increasing number of zeros on it. They are not only goal-scoring but money-making machines – just another game in which everyone wants to be the winner. *Forbes* magazine has the Portuguese in the lead, at least for the moment, earning 53 million dollars a year in salary and bonuses. On top of that there's a nice bit of sponsorship cash which amounted to 29 million dollars in 2015, making a dizzying 82 million dollars a year. CR7 is not only the highest paid footballer on the planet for the third year running, he is now the top earner across all team sports worldwide.

If the figures are correct – although it's difficult to verify in the opaque world of football – Leo Messi is in second place. The Argentine ears 51 million dollars in salary and bonuses, plus 26 million in sponsorship deals. He brings in around 5 million less a year than CR7, but they both significantly outstrip Zlatan Ibrahimović, who is in third place with 37 million dollars in 2015. And fourth place goes to … Neymar Júnior. It's surprising how quickly the Brazilian has made his way up the ranks of this exclusive club.

Cristiano had already made financial headlines on 11 June 2009, when Man United officially confirmed on their website that they had accepted Real's 94 million euro (£80 million) offer to buy the striker – and noted that it was a world record price for a footballer. He now tops the list of most expensive players in history, overtaking Zinedine Zidane's 75 million euro transfer from Juventus to Real in 2001, Kaká's 65 million euro move from AC Milan to Real in 2009, and Luís Figo's 61 million euro transfer from Barça to Real in 2000.

The figure forked out by Real causes quite a stir – some see it as positive for the game, while others are against the spending of such an extravagant amount. Former British minister for sport and tourism, Gerry Sutcliffe, admits he is concerned about the sustainability of the game. 'These teams are big businesses now and this type of money is around but we've got to make sure that there's … sustainability for this because we don't want to see clubs go to the wall.'

'These transfers are a serious challenge to the idea of fair play and the concept of financial balance in our competitions,' declares former UEFA president Michel Platini, who considers Real Madrid's offer excessive and 'very disconcerting at a time when football faces some of its most serious financial challenges'. By contrast, former FIFA president Joseph Blatter praises such deals: 'This is an example of a fantastic investment – there may be a global financial crisis, but football is still on the rise.' In Spain, Barça vice-president and director of marketing Jaume Ferrer insists that 'there is no player in the world worth 94 million euros', explaining that the figure is 'not in line with the current market. When you pay such high prices it allows other clubs to demand enormous figures. It can cause a sharp inflation in the market.'

Real Madrid president Florentino Pérez puts an end to the debate: 'The signings that seem the most expensive are in fact the cheapest.' What does he mean by that? Former Real Madrid general manager Jorge Valdano clarifies: 'Cristiano is an unbelievable footballer. We paid what we did because it's worth it – we'll make it all back, with interest. It's an investment in a club which is in the business of putting on a great performance. Having Cristiano Ronaldo brings a global market to our doorstep. And in a time of crisis, that guarantees us economic potential that we wouldn't otherwise have.' Everyone at the club agrees – the directors are convinced that the millions spent on Ronaldo are a worthwhile investment that will lead to a sold out Bernabéu, summer tours, TV rights, merchandising and increased sponsorship.

Forbes can vouch for that. According to the magazine, although the two stars earn infinitely more than everyone else, one has to take into account that they score so many goals and create even more. And that can only serve to line the coffers of their respective clubs, which, incidentally, are the two most valuable in the world. In short, it's worth paying the price for them.

So what does the man in question think? 'I realise it's got people talking, but it makes me feel proud to be the most expensive player in footballing history.'

* * *

When Neymar Júnior is presented at Barcelona on 3 June 2013, club president Bartomeu – who was then vice-president – tells the assembled press: 'Neymar cost us 57 million euros, more than we envisaged paying for his transfer [40 million]. This was due to the interest from other clubs, which pushed up the price. We must also take into account that the player has come here a year earlier than originally intended. The proceeds of the sale are shared between four entities:

DIS, Teisa, N&N Sports and Santos – with no fees to agents or intermediaries, as is our custom.' The confidentiality clause means he cannot reveal exactly how the money has been divided. The quoted figure means Neymar is now the second-largest purchase in Barça history, behind Ibrahimović. But all Bartomeu will say is that 10 million euros have been paid up front, and the rest will be paid in three years' time to the four companies that own the rights to the player. There are plenty of questions on the issue of the transfer fee, but that's the only official response.

Nonetheless, it will remain a hot topic of debate both in Spain and Brazil. Sources close to the deal claim the fee is higher – between 70 and 75 million euros, and that 32 million is said to have gone to Santos. And that, they say, is without counting the amount Barça paid to play two friendlies against Santos, one at the Nou Camp and one in Brazil, as well as nearly 8 million euros paid as an option on three other Peixe youngsters: Victor Andrade, Gabriel and Giva. It is claimed 20 million has gone to N&N – Neymar Pai's company – and the rest has been shared between DIS and Teisa. But Real Madrid president Pérez has an even higher figure. He claims he passed up the opportunity to buy the Brazilian player because it would allegedly have cost the club 150 million euros.

The debate intensifies over the coming months, descending into what is later referred to as

'Neymargate'. On 5 December 2013, Barça club member Jordi Cases brings a lawsuit against club president Sandro Rosell, alleging that the actual amount paid for the Brazilian forward was more than 57 million euros, and that Rosell allegedly misappropriated funds.

On 10 January 2014, the national court's public prosecutor requests that the case be heard, and FIFA is asked to provide documentation of the transfer and various relevant contracts. Three days later, Barcelona officially request that the case not come before the court. But on 22 January, Judge Pablo Ruz agrees to hear the lawsuit, and nine different contracts dated between November 2011–September 2013 are to be considered as part of the investigation. The following day, Rosell resigns over what he terms an 'unfair and reckless' accusation. Bartomeu takes the reins at Barça and now has to explain the various details of Neymar's signing. He admits that the total cost of the transfer was in fact 86.2 million euros, rather than the 57.1 million originally stated, although he says this included the cost of Neymar's departure relating to the transfer. Forty million euros was paid to N&N and 17.1 million to Santos. Barça also signed a separate agreement relating to options on three youth academy players, worth 7.9 million euros, as well as a new contract with N&N to monitor the youngsters' development – 400,000 euros a year for five years, a total of 2 million. In the end, Neymar will have cost 56.7 million in total, 11.3 million per season, but the additional salaries, commissions and payments take the total to 86.2 million, excluding any possible bonus.

Despite the lack of transparency when it comes to footballers' salaries, *Forbes* has the Brazilian's annual earnings at 36 million dollars: 14 million in salary and bonuses, and 22 million in sponsorship income. For one thing, Neymar is the only footballer who earns more off the pitch than on. What's more, each of his goals is worth around 250,000 dollars.

Meanwhile, the figures have certainly given Spanish football fans plenty to talk about, and across the country the debate continues about the bubble of the football world during a time of economic crisis.

* * *

Record transfer fees were not on the cards when Leo Messi joined the Barcelona youth academy at the tender age of thirteen. But more than thirteen years on, he is clearly worth a great deal to the club.

Sports marketing company Euromericas has produced a report about the Messi brand using data gathered over the last five years. The conclusion is impressive, claiming Messi is worth 400 million euros. Euromericas CEO Gerardo Molina claims that 'Leo's media impact is five times that of Cristiano's. And according to a diverse range of studies, Cristiano is worth between 150 and 160 million euros'.

Of course, this could change overnight: a new title win could switch up the order. Cristiano Ronaldo is the most searched footballer on Google España, and sooner or later that will have an impact on the bank balance. It's about more than just football, as Valdano points out, it's about entertainment. And you can't put a price on dreams.

In other words, the eternal duel continues.

This is football, recession style.

Chapter 14

Branding

'Nowadays, Messi, Ronaldo and Neymar are global enterprises in a market where agents find them the most lucrative opportunities,' opines Patrick Mignon, sociologist at the National Institute of Sport and Physical Education in Paris.

'A top player is like a Louis Vuitton bag or a Cartier ring,' adds Gunter Gebauer, professor of philosophy at the Institute for Sports Science at the University of Hanover. 'They are a marketable brand of their own.'

There is no doubt that Messi, Ronaldo and Neymar have cross-border and mass audience appeal as advertising icons and brand ambassadors. Dozens of companies feature them in adverts, publicity material and campaigns to raise awareness and break into new markets.

First, the sports brands ...

A football-shaped meteor has fallen somewhere on earth. Cristiano receives a call: 'The boots have arrived.' He leaps into them and he is transformed. He is a superhero capable of galactic speeds. He can leap from building to building like Spiderman. He has the city at his feet. After a few circuits around the globe he lands on the pitch at the Bernabéu. And all thanks to Nike. The global sports giant has spared no expense in riding the media tidal wave with this particular advert, which premieres in the lead-up to one of the most hyped matches in football: the Real Madrid-Barça Clásico on 25 October 2015. CR7 is a safe bet for Nike, who know that everything he touches turns to gold. It's much the same with Neymar, another of the company's big ambassadors.

Meanwhile … Adidas favours Leo. After a long legal battle, the German sports giant won Messi from Nike, which had sponsored him since he was fourteen years old. He signed an extremely lucrative contract with Adidas in 2006, just before the Germany World Cup.

And it's not just about trainers. There are millions at stake in this branding battle. Cristiano's Nike deal extends to a clothing line with the slogan, 'Love to win, hate to lose'. And Nike has made him its standard-bearer for the 2014 Brazil World Cup – running the risk that, had Portugal not qualified, Cristiano's absence from the action could have cost the American company an estimated $14 million.

Then there are the videogames and billboards. Messi is on the DVD cover of FIFA 16, Cristiano is on Pro Evolution Soccer 2013, while Neymar appears on the 2016 cover. The Brazilian is also an ambassador for Panasonic, among other things. 'Our brand has enjoyed a huge leap in popularity thanks to Neymar,' Panasonic executive director Takumi Kajisha said recently. 'He has done a lot for us in Brazil, and his arrival in Barcelona could benefit us on a global scale, because Barça is well known in Asia and Africa. As an ambassador, he could achieve even more success in those markets.'

And let's not forget the drinks. Leo was the face of Pepsi in its 'Live for now' and 'Live for football' global campaigns during the 2014 World Cup, in which the Argentine has fun doing tricks with a drinks can. Back in 2006, CR7 played football with ice cubes for Coke's World Cup campaign targeted at the Chinese market. Then he moved on to energy drink Soccerade, publicising its Lemon-Lime, Ice Blue and Fruit Burst flavours. Neymar, meanwhile, is sponsored by Red Bull and Guaraná Antárctica. In the advert for the fruit-flavoured soft drink, he is seen lounging in a deck-chair on a Brazilian beach, popping open a can. 'Are you heading off to Europe?' asks a friend. 'Europe?' he ponders, picturing himself playing football on snow-covered fields and freezing, deserted beaches, where the man in the little fish and chip shack has no idea what Guaraná is. 'Not right now,' he tells his friend. 'Beach, sun and Guaraná are all I need.'

And the banks. Portugal's Banco Espirito Santo was Cristiano's first big sponsor, when he was just a promising eighteen-year-old and the trophies and prizes were a future dream. The investment bank picked him to front its campaigns just less than a year before UEFA Euro 2004 in Portugal. 'We think the joy of the game and the spectacle are the best part of football,' explains Paulo Padrão, the bank's director of marketing. 'Cristiano Ronaldo is incomparable when it comes to representing the game in that way. He is a young Portuguese icon – proof that if you combine talent and hard work, you can succeed.' Neymar was the face of Banco Santander in Brazil in an alliance between 'the current best footballer in Brazil and the best bank in the world', as described by former company president Emilio Botín.

In the fashion stakes, Leo has worked with Dolce & Gabbana for many years, donning the Italian design-ers' famously loud suits for various Ballon d'Or galas. More recently he has worn Armani, a brand for which CR7 has also modelled underwear, and where he met his ex, Irina Shayk, during a campaign. And who could forget the black and white 'housekeeping' advert, in which he searches for his shirt in a hotel room while a maid hides to watch him topless, which garnered plenty of attention. And following the success of his Armani underwear campaign he decided to launch his own brand and line, the CR7 Underwear and Socks Collection – another opportunity to show off his mus-cles. Not to be left behind, Neymar has also been seen sporting underwear for Brazilian brand Lupo, and has recently launched a line of Rock & Soda trousers and long denim shorts targeted at young shoppers.

The three players sell and promote everything from jeans, sportswear, trainers and underwear to cars, aftershave, sweets, toys, phones, TVs, airlines, watches, comics, shampoo and instant messaging services. Their list of sponsors is impressive to say the least:

Neymar: Nike, Red Bull, Volkswagen, Replay, Gillette & Rexona, Panasonic, Listerine, Claro, Tenys Pé, Lupo, Guaraná Antárctica, Heliar batteries.

Ronaldo: Nike, Altice, Abbott, Herbalife, TAG Heuer, PokerStars, Sacoor Brothers, Clear, XTrade, Monster, Sixpad Training Gear.

Messi: Adidas, Pepsi, Gatorade, Lays, FIFA 16, Gillette, Ooredoo, EA Sports, Tata Motors, Space Scooter, Armani, Huawei.

But what sorts of values do the players' brands represents? What image are they selling? What qualities speak to a global audience?

Neymar is synonymous with fun, daring and life in the fast lane. He is a young, friendly kid, with extravagant hair and tattoos, in tune with technology, music and fashion, and highly visible on Facebook, Twitter and Instagram. Since 2010, both his former club Santos and the player's NRJ brand have emphasised these characteristics to attract sponsors. And it seems to have worked well. *SportsPro* magazine says he is the most saleable sportsman with the highest marketing value in the world – they rank him above golfer Rory McIlroy, Messi and Olympian Usain Bolt, although his sponsors have occasionally had to pull him up on his behaviour off the pitch, fearful that the negative image projected by late night partying will eventually impact on their brands. 'He's a young, successful foot-baller, who plays for a great team. That's why he's so attractive to commercial brands. Neymar is a business,' say the sports marketing experts.

With his six pack on display, Cristiano is depicted as the masculine sex symbol, fulfilling the Greek ideal of beauty and health. But competitiveness and hard work, professionalism and a desire to 'perform' are also key facets of his brand – the will to win and gain respect. In addition, the Real star is a natural communicator, extremely comfortable in front of the camera. He does not bat an eyelid at being made up, posing for long photo shoots, and repeating the same movements over and over for the camera. He enjoys playing the starring role. A set, for him, is just an extension of the football pitch, where he is always number one. It's just another form of perfor-mance, albeit a little different from what he does every weekend. And because of that, he approaches promoting trainers with the same determination as he would making a run at goal.

In fact, Ronaldo's commitment to his sponsors often seems to go above and beyond his contractual obligations – like when he had a disagreement with his former Real team-mate Xabi Alonso over whether Adidas or Nike made the best football boots. They were in a training session at the beginning of 2014, when the midfielder, who now plays at Bayern Munich, criticised the fact that the Portuguese wore 'plastic' trainers made by a 'basketball brand'. Ronaldo froze in astonishment at what he was hearing, before waving his arms wildly, insisting that these were the shoes of a star player. It was a small private disagreement that happened to be captured by a TV camera, but it could almost have been a scripted advert. Funnily enough, at the time he was also wearing a sweatshirt made by Adidas, which sponsors Real Madrid.

So, what does Leo Messi sell? 'Authenticity,' claims Fernando Solanas, head of sport marketing at Adidas Iberia. Fair enough, but what is his appeal off the pitch? 'He is just, quite simply, himself, a guy who loves being with his family, his friends, his people. Too often sportsmen seem to live in a distant universe, very far removed from our world. Leo, with his shyness, is close to all football fans.' But it's more than that. From early on in his professional career, the image of Messi was that of a boy who succeeded in reaching the top despite his height and growth problems. With hard work, perseverance and strong will, he has demonstrated and continues to demonstrate to the wider world that nothing is impossible.

Messi does not have the same self-assuredness and ease in front of the camera, nor the same physique or demeanour as Cristiano Ronaldo.

Nonetheless, he's game for anything, even modelling underwear for Dolce & Gabbana. After all, he also has muscles worth flaunting. And his appeal is obvious in a series of promos filmed with NBA star Kobe Bryant for Turkish Airlines, which were a resounding success. In the first, in 2012, they compete to see who can do the most tricks with the ball to entertain a little boy who is on a plane journey with them – an advert that garnered more than 112 million Youtube views. And the second, 'Kobe vs Messi: The Selfie Shootout', filmed towards the end of 2013, was named by Youtube as the 'Ad of the decade'. In it, the two sports stars travel round the world trying to take more and more impressive selfies in unusual and exotic places, garnering a cool 144 million hits, and even seeing Bryant photobombing Leo in Istanbul. The LA Lakers star is a huge Barça fan and has even spoken of wanting to finish his career playing for the Barcelona basketball team. In 2014 the airline substitutes Bryant with Chelsea star Didier Drogba, who flies around the world trying to find ever more remote and exotic restaurants to eat at, always spotting a photo on the wall that reveals Messi got there first. Yet another funny ad that has racked up more than 63 million views.

It's clear that Messi, Neymar and Ronaldo can sell pretty much anything, in any corner of the world. Their faces are instantly recognisable. And there is no better example of that than the fact that Ronaldo has decided to sell 50 per cent of all his image rights to Singaporean tycoon Peter Lim, the largest shareholder of Primera División club Valencia, who is also a personal friend of Ronaldo's agent Jorge Mendes. CR7 announces the deal on his Facebook page: 'I am very excited to announce my latest deal with Mint Media, owned by my good friend, businessman Peter Lim from Singapore, to acquire my image rights. This is a very strategic move for me and my management team to take the Cristiano Ronaldo brand to the next level, especially in Asia.' The owner of the other 50 per cent of his image rights is, of course, Real Madrid, which also has a special interest in the Asian market and has already organised several summer tours around the continent. The more global fans, the more the club can make in rights and marketing. Everything is analysed, everything is part of a carefully measured strategy. It's yet another competition in which nothing can be left to chance.

Chapter 15

Social media

With more than 116 million 'Likes', Cristiano is the undisputed king of Facebook, the most popular person in the world. The Real Madrid player knocked singer Shakira off the top spot in March 2015, and no one has been able to catch him since then. It's a similar story on Twitter, where he has 43 million followers. He is the top sportsman on the social network, and fourteenth overall, behind global stars such as Katy Perry, Justin Bieber and Taylor Swift.

His online success doesn't end there. On 23 February 2016, he became the first athlete to gain a total of 200 million followers across Facebook, Twitter and Instagram, according to Hookit, an analytics platform that measures sportsmen and women's social media activity and exposure. And he has been gaining around 135,000 new fans every day. The man himself show his gratitude in 140 characters: 'Really proud to be the 1st athlete with 200 million social media followers. A big thank you to all my fans!' he tweets, adding a string of emoticons showing happiness and thanks.

One place and 78 million followers behind him is Leo Messi – a significant feat considering the Argentine still doesn't have a Twitter account. In third place is NBA basketball star LeBron James.

In 2013 CR7's online magnetism prompted him to launch his own community, vivaronaldo.com, a free site and app in English where fans could interact and keep up with the latest news on their idol. Users could follow all Cristiano's matches and enter competitions to win signed shirts or tickets to watch him play. They could also view exclusive photos and videos of events, connect with other fans, and interact with the player himself. The venture came to an end in the autumn of 2015 – but not due to a lack of success. The company behind the site promises to return with renewed force: 'It's been a thrilling experience to power up such an amazing community of Cristiano fans for the last two and a half years. You can all keep supporting Cristiano on Viva Ronaldo's Facebook, Twitter and Instagram accounts. Thank you for being the Best Fans in the World! Stay tuned for the incredible products we're already developing. They will allow you to live and share your passions like never before!' reads the homepage.

This is one area where Lionel Messi, with his 'mere' 85 million Facebook followers, can't compete with his biggest rival. The number 10 was the fifth Barça player to create a page on the site, after Gerard

Piqué, Andrés Iniesta, David Villa and Pedro. The launch was officially announced in April 2011 via the Barcelona Twitter account, and within hours his page was flooded with fans. He has yet to create his own Twitter profile, however. There are plenty bearing his name and picture, but his family and friends have had to step in on more than one occasion to confirm that they are not official accounts. As his sister María Sol has tweeted in the past: 'A message from Leo! "Once again I would like to clarify that I do not have a Twitter account and I don't intend to create one for now. If I did, I would announce it via my Facebook page. I hope this clarifies things so that people don't get misled by any accounts that contain my name."'

But there is another Messi on Twitter: Matías Messi, Leo's brother. His tweets have caused quite a stir among football fans – for example, by asking why Real fans follow him if they dislike him so much. And although he clarified that he wasn't talking about all Whites fans, the debate was already underway. He also caused a commotion when he posted a picture comparing Leo and Cristiano's various titles dating back to 2009.

Social networks are clearly just another battle-ground for the world's biggest sports stars, or at least for their fans. It's a global contest that shows no sign of abating. It begins to build up just before a match or before an award such as the FIFA Ballon d'Or, and it gets particularly intense around a derby, when players are the subject of a torrent of insults alongside assurances of undying support. There are declarations of eternal love and hatred, commentary, analyses, articles, campaigns for and against. The web is a free-for-all where everyone has an opinion, and football – which leads the way in online sports chatter – sparks passionate debate. And although it's a team sport, it is the individual stars who command a lot of the attention online. Cristiano has far more Facebook followers than the official Real Madrid page (90 million), whereas Messi is a bit behind the Barcelona page (93 million). Even Neymar is not doing badly: he has almost 57 million Facebook fans, more than 22 million on Twitter 51 million on Instagram.

And that's not counting all the football lovers who follow all the fake accounts of their idols, of which there has been an explosion in recent years. In October 2013, Neymar decided to use the same background on his Facebook and Twitter page and link one to the other to avoid confusion with any fake profiles. The Barça player is particularly active online, continually sharing news about his life or biblical verses. He tweets far more than many of his fellow players. And barely a day goes by without him posting photos to Instagram – with his friends, his father, his son, his teammates, sticking out his tongue, playing the piano or jumping on the bed.

The sporting elite have found a way to boost their personal profile and brand in a global, immediate and cost-effective way. The key is the opportunity to share moments of their lives beyond the matches, training sessions and other public appearances. Within minutes their photos, opinions and messages are seen, read, commented on and reposted by millions of followers around the world, enabling them to close the gap between them and mere mortals.

When Cristiano Ronaldo tweets to say how he is or that Real are going to win, or he shares his holiday snaps, his fans get to feel he is conversing with them and they can respond to him directly. In reality, it's part of a well-oiled marketing juggernaut that tells the stories of the players' lives and reinforces their brand every day thanks to the power of the web.

Acknowledgements

I would like to thank Duncan Heath, Nira Begum, Robert Sharman, Sheli Rodney, Laure Merle d'Aubigné and Roberto Domínguez and Estela Celada.

This is dedicated to Olmo, Lorenzo, Elvira, Alda and Tullio.